ADMINISTRATORS AT RISK:

TOOLS AND TECHNOLOGIES FOR SECURING YOUR FUTURE

JAMIESON A. McKENZIE

NATIONAL EDUCATIONAL SERVICE

BLOOMINGTON, INDIANA

EDITED BY DAVID M. RUETSCHLIN
PHI DELTA KAPPA
BLOOMINGTON, INDIANA

COVER DESIGN BY BRYAN THATCHER

PRINTED IN THE UNITED STATES OF AMERICA

ISBN 1-879639-27-0

TABLE OF CONTENTS

TABLE OF CONTENTS (CONTINUED)

TABLE OF CONTENTS (CONTINUED)

ABOUT THE AUTHOR

A graduate of Yale, Columbia University, and Rutgers University, Dr. Jamieson A. McKenzie combines his experience as a former superintendent with his expertise in technology and managing change to provide professional consulting for schools who are entering the process of change. He has presented workshops on technology and planning for the National School Boards Association, American Association of School Administrators, Association for Supervision and Curriculum Development, Council for Exceptional Children, and Apple, as well as numerous school districts across the country. He has also published *From Now On,* a monthly electronic technology newsletter which reaches school districts through AppleLink. Dr. McKenzie is the author of several publications on educational technology, site-based management, and parental involvement in education. His articles have appeared in the *Staff Development Journal, Executive Educator, The School Administrator,* and *American School Boards Journal.*

FOREWORD

"They just don't get it" has become an all too common admonition of the 1990s. Rapidly changing industries, values, and economic structures have left thousands of factory workers, computer salespeople, soldiers, and aerospace engineers unemployed and confused. They just didn't understand that things wouldn't—and *shouldn't*—remain as they always had been.

Educators, as a group, are no different from the people in all those other enterprises who believed that change would be incremental if it happened at all. Those who believe they can survive through incremental change are due for a rude awakening. They don't get it. Schools are about to undergo the same kind of change that has revolutionized almost every aspect of Western society. Many educators will soon find themselves unemployed or underemployed without understanding why.

Jamieson McKenzie has explained why, and has even provided a handbook for those willing to face the future and change. The author's assumptions are clearly stated and assertions are clearly documented. From telephones to teacher training, from new school construction to parent conferences, McKenzie has laid out a blueprint for operating a twenty-first century school. The research is cited and discussed. The conceptual framework is defined according to accepted literature and placed in context. Yet in spite of all that, *Administrators*

At Risk: Tools and Technologies for Securing Your Future is not your typical education book. The conventions may be familiar, but the content is very unconventional. Indeed, any educator who wants to do a good job, or simply survive into the next decade, should read, study, and implement the concepts in this book.

I am confident that hundreds, or even thousands, of educators will read this book and make crucial adjustments in beliefs and practices which will benefit an untold number of children, in addition to prolonging their own careers. Some schools will be designed differently and equipped differently, and some students will be subject to new and more meaningful expectations based on a technologically complex world.

Some educators may not learn about this book and will not have the opportunity to use its advice. Some will know about the book and elect not to read it. Some will read it but decide to do nothing.

It is really too bad that some educators will miss this book; it is sad that some will read it but do nothing. Our students desperately need new opportunities and new expectations. Our society needs better-educated citizens and workers. The information is here just when educators need it most.

I guess some people just don't get it.

> —Michael F. Sullivan
> Executive Director
> Agency for Instructional Technology

INTRODUCTION

We are witnessing the final phase of "smokestack education," an outmoded approach to schooling that was designed to fuel an industrial society's need for assembly-line workers. The new Information Age promises to transform how people learn about their world. New technologies are likely to revolutionize the ways individuals gain insight and make meaning.

Even though our schools have been flooded with new technologies during the past decade, the educational practices, rituals, and beliefs associated with an industrial society have blunted the potential of those technologies to open classrooms to the new world. A host of attitudes and behaviors have combined to mold the uses of new equipment to match familiar images and traditions.

But the old ways of educating children are increasingly inadequate and irrelevant. What is needed is an educational system that challenges all students to do their own thinking. Business leaders, clergy, futurists, and others now recognize this and are united in their desire to see a generation of students emerge as imaginative, inventive, and collaborative problem-solvers.

Administrators At Risk offers a vision of an educational future unfettered by the smokestack paradigm. It originally appeared as a collection of essays in *From Now On*, a monthly electronic newsletter available on *AppleLink* to school districts across the nation.

Behind all of these essays is a belief in the value of teaching children to ask their own questions and the potential of new technologies to support such independent questioning. This belief is fundamental to the future of a democratic society.

These essays call on the reader to leave the "comfort zone" and to take a hero's journey of discovery and adventure. The journey requires us to re-invent our schools. It offers many trials along the way; but it also promises the possibility of illumination, insight, and transcendence.

CHAPTER ONE

INNOVATION VS. STABILITY IN ORGANIZATIONS: WHAT PRICE CHANGE?

PART ONE:
JACK-IN-THE-BOX IS NO LONGER JUST A CHILDHOOD TOY

Life in the 1990s is full of surprises, startling shifts that often leave us disoriented. We live in a topsy-turvy world, with Jack-in-the-Boxes popping open all around us. No matter where one turns, the workplace skills of yesterday are being shelved as new technologies and a global economy require new ways of operating and communicating.

But there is steadfast, and apparently growing, resistance to change. Adult workers find their middle years—years which once promised serenity and the pleasure of consolidating the benefits of a well-established career—disturbed by the *chaos* of modern society. Corporate take-overs and economic downturns have undermined job security; millions have found themselves out on the street after decades of loyal service. New owners, intent on the bottom line, are quick to send workers packing. Loyalty counts for little, and seniority quickly becomes a deficit.

"But what technology skills do you have?" employers ask. Suddenly looking for a new job, the aging secretary wishes she had grumbled less and learned more when her company first introduced new technologies. "Out there in the job market, it's what you know and can do that counts," laments one unhappy job-seeker. "They don't care how many years you have put in."

Faith Popcorn (1991) claims that the *cocooning* of the 1980s is turning into *burrowing*; Americans are pulling inward, seeking enclaves, and avoiding the sound and fury of society. In *The Popcorn Report*, she identifies *downshifting* as a major trend of this decade. Many successful people are stepping off the merry-go-round in search of simpler, less frantic experiences and careers.

Negative report after negative report claim that schools are failing to prepare students for this turbulent and surprising world, but educators seem seriously divided and confused over how to respond. Most schools seem content to dominate the "trailing edge" of the changing society. Major segments burrow even deeper into the trenches, avoiding change or indulging in meaningless tinkering. Whole districts stumble into the future. Others dash from trend to trend without creating any lasting and significant benefits for students. Bandwagons go roaring through with great promises, hefty price tags, and few dividends.

While school people rush about or burrow deeper, others plan the equivalent of corporate take-overs. One need only listen to the radio to hear the new ventures nipping at the schools. How often do we hear ads for Sylvan Learning Centers or *Hooked on Phonics*? They are aiming at the market niches that the schools have failed to fill.

"We can do it better and faster and make the client happier," these entrepreneurs claim. They market their products with skills few public school people possess or understand. And frustrated parents and children will flock to these new educational programs in the same way they flock to a new shopping mall, a new restaurant, or a new movie theater.

And Whittle Communications! Who would have thought that 10,000 school systems would allow *Channel One* into their classrooms with daily doses of advertising? "It will never catch on!" I remember hearing.

Chris Whittle met with great resistance when he first came up with the highly successful *Channel One* program in the late Eighties. He offered schools free televisions for every classroom, free satellite dishes, and free daily news broadcasts. In return, he asked for the right to include several minutes of commercials in these programs. Despite the early resistance, many schools embraced the advertising in order to benefit from the free technology.

Now Whittle is planning a thousand new American schools, designed to compete with existing public schools.

Smokestack schools beware! If you do not quickly find a way to reach your clients, there may soon be more competition than you are prepared to handle. Powerful forces will force us into a free market in which educational funding flows to those who make the clients happy. In this brave new educational world, underachieving schools will shut down and cease operating, just as restaurants and retail stores have always done if they failed to "turn a profit." Teachers in these schools will find themselves seeking jobs in a marketplace that asks, "But what technology skills do you have? What instructional skills have you mastered in recent years? How flexible are you? Do you like to work on teams? Are you willing to keep learning?"

New schools will pop up all around us if we do not reach our clients soon. They will be lean and ferocious in their pursuit of market share. Survival in this new educational marketplace will depend on a major shift in educational planning and performance. Schools that cling to the past may find themselves working with a shrinking client base; and teachers who fail to acquire Information Age skills may find themselves, like workers for Sears and IBM, forced into an earlier retirement than planned.

PART TWO:
BALANCING STABILITY WITH INNOVATION

Systems theory argues that healthy organizations provide a balance between *stability* and *innovation*. A degree of stability is essential if performance is to be strong. If the rate and level of change is too high, people lose their balance and performance suffers. People within the organization need some degree of predictability and certainty. If rules and procedures are unclear, anxiety will reduce effectiveness.

At the same time, organizations can invest too heavily in stability, thereby cutting off or ignoring messages from outside the organization about the need for changes. If the organization fails to heed these messages and to monitor changing conditions, it may not move swiftly enough to adjust its operations. This failure can result in obsolescence and even extinction.

Commitment to some appropriate level of innovation protects the organization from obsolescence and extinction. In this sense, *innovation* really means *adaptation*—responsible shifts in practice to meet changing conditions. At a minimum, an organization should devote resources to interpreting outside pressures and developments. Instead of ignoring and blocking such messages, the organization designates people to scan the horizon and keep a lookout for new developments, new threats, and new possibilities. Some people are charged with "thinking the unthinkable," so that they can prepare the group for unlikely but plausible events.

Growth and adaptation require a commitment to organizational development. As new developments arise, someone must be responsible for figuring out how the organization may respond while maintaining a reasonable level of stability.

4

How does your School District Rate on this Issue of Stability and Innovation?

This survey was designed to help you measure the commitment of your organization to managing the future. It is an organizational assessment tool, which might be helpful in guiding you toward those changes and plans that will prepare your schools for a turbulent and often surprising environment. The goal is to create reflective thinking about ways to intensify organizational commitment to innovation, adaptability and growth. The survey should be given to various groups in the school, including administrators, the district technology committee, the school council, and others.

The Innovation and Environmental Scanning Index

State to what extent each of the following statements tends to be descriptive of your organization.

1. We have a staff member who is clearly identified as responsible for keeping an eye on the horizon, scanning newspapers, magazines, and current information of all kinds to keep us on the alert.

   __definitely __to some extent __not really __not at all

2. Discussion about the future and various emerging trends rarely occurs during meetings, because our attention is devoted to today, tomorrow, and next week.

   __definitely __to some extent __not really__not at all

3. We are very clear about our strategies to keep customers from running to our competition, and we do a thorough and ongoing job of listening to our customers.

   __definitely __to some extent __not really__not at all

5

4. We have discussed most of Tucker's "Driving Forces" (see discussion on pages 8 to 21) within the past year (speed, convenience, age waves, choice, lifestyle, discounting, value-adding, customer service, techno-edge, quality).

    __definitely __to some extent __not really__not at all

5. We have inverted the organizational chart to put the customer at the top, with service people and front-line employees next, all for the purpose of emphasizing listening and getting close to the customer's needs.

    __definitely __to some extent __not really__not at all

6. New ideas and unusual solutions to problems are encouraged and rewarded in a highly conscious manner, with all employees aware that "idea champions" are treated well.

    __definitely __to some extent __not really__not at all

7. We have no real formal way of measuring how employees feel about working in our organization—whether, for example, they believe that new ideas really are welcome.

    __definitely __to some extent __not really__not at all

8. We have no real competition.

    __definitely __to some extent __not really__not at all

9. We commit a substantial part of our budget each year to training our staff in problem-solving, customer service, and other skills that might give us a competitive edge.

    __definitely __to some extent __not really__not at all

10. Looking ahead 5 to 10 years takes up a good deal of our time.

    __definitely __to some extent __not really__not at all

SCORING THE INNOVATION AND ENVIRONMENTAL SCANNING INDEX

The scoring of your responses is fairly simple. Compare your answers with the chart below to determine how many points you have scored.

	definitely	to some extent	not really	not at all
1.	+2	+1	-1	-2
2.	-2	-1	+1	+2
3.	+2	+1	-1	-2
4.	+2	+1	-1	-2
5.	+2	+1	-1	-2
6.	+2	+1	-1	-2
7.	-2	-1	+1	+2
8.	-2	-1	+1	+2
9.	+2	+1	-1	-2
10.	+2	+1	-1	-2

Total Points:		
	-20	In Severe Need of Future Thinking
	-10	Behind the Times
	0	In Neutral
	+10	Committed to Future Thinking
	+20	Clairvoyant

Once you have administered the survey, discuss the implications. Might your organization modify its "infra-structure" to be directed more to the future? The goal is to create reflective thinking about ways to intensify organizational commitment to innovation, adaptability, and growth.

Are we like the dinosaurs of old? Are we incapable of adjusting to a changing climate and changing conditions? Do we have the institutional wherewithal to convert good intentions into effective action? Is there a sufficient balance between stability and innovation? Or are we lopsided, too weighted in one extreme or another?

PART THREE:
MONITORING THE DRIVING FORCES OF CHANGE

Tucker (1991) identifies ten major social forces that organizations need to consider when planning how to meet their clients' needs and interests.

1. Speed

2. Convenience

3. Age Waves

4. Choice

5. Lifestyle

6. Discounting

7. Value-Adding

8. Customer Service

9. Techno-edge

10. Quality

According to Tucker, many people's choices and market decisions will be made with these issues in mind—even when it comes to schooling for their children.

One of the side-effects of enhanced information technology has been expanded consumer power. In earlier decades it was difficult to know what consumers wanted. The sheer task of collecting and interpreting data was overwhelming. As a result, decisions about consumer preferences were based more on hunches and focus groups than on day-to-day trend analysis. Major shifts in preferences were discernible over seasons and months, but it was difficult to see daily and weekly shifts. Strategies were designed "on high" by top management.

With barcodes and daily data collection, the consumer has gained enormous influence; and the marketplace rules have changed dramatically. Successful companies are the ones with the skill and equipment to figure out in advance what the consumer will want today and respond with a customized response in time to meet the customer at the door with what they had in mind.

The race now goes to those who listen to the customer most carefully and most skillfully, adjusting their strategies and performance to meet what they have learned.

SPEED

Tucker provides examples of organizations, such as Federal Express, that have capitalized on consumers' desire to "have it now or yesterday." If you run out of printer supplies and need them immediately in order to get a report to the Board by tomorrow, try to buy these supplies locally. Many times they will be out of stock.

"We can get it for you in 7 to 10 days," they mumble.

"No thanks," you reply, turning to your copy of *MacUser* and an ad you remember for a mail-order supply house.

"We can have it to you by 10:00 a.m. tomorrow morning," they purr reassuringly from the far-away state of Washington, "as long as you are willing to pay an extra $18 surcharge for Federal Express."

The sum seems small compared with the embarrassment of showing up at the meeting without your overhead transparencies. Of course, you learn to keep extra supplies to avoid such extravagances in the future; but from then on, you probably will give your business to the Washington firm, rather than to the smokestack business in town.

Industry is excited about such concepts as "real time" inventory, which takes advantage of superior information to direct a flow of parts toward the factory and finished products toward the customer to minimize shelf time and costly inventory. In the future, "real time" inventory may allow an automobile company to finish Mrs. Smith's new sports car before she has even decided to buy it. Careful forecasting of previous buyer behaviors allows the computer to order a red item with just the kinds of equipment Mrs. Smith would love to see in a car. One morning, when she wakes up determined to cruise down to the showroom to see what they have available, a truck pulls into the dealer's lot and begins to unload a red sports car.

"Mrs. Smith," beams the salesperson, "We were expecting you and I think you'll love this new red car we have for you."

"It's exactly what I had in mind," Mrs. Smith smiles. "How did you know I wanted a stick shift?"

The salesperson winks. "The magic of technology!"

What does SPEED have to do with schools?

Currently, schools make relatively poor use of time. Frequently, teachers assign laborious practice items to large groups of students, regardless of whether their learning and skill levels will be enhanced by completing the assignment. Schools are not at all reluctant to condemn students to long hours of tedium and drudgery that have little to do with student outcomes. Teachers dole out ditto page after ditto page to entire classes, without customizing or adapting them to individual needs.

On the other hand, it sometimes seems as if we are speeding through curriculum material at breakneck pace, especially when we are handed thick science or social studies texts—biology and world history being prime examples—that require a "nine-month dash" to go from cover to cover. "No time for thinking in this class! No time for student questions! We have a lot to cover."

And then we have the school lunch line. A generation raised on fast food often waits in line for as long as 10 minutes during a 25-minute lunch period. Small wonder participation rates have dropped in many districts.

How long does it take to get a paper back in high school? Good teachers are prompt. Some wait weeks, long past the waning of student interest and enthusiasm. Some retain papers and tests "for their files."

How long must a parent spend waiting for someone to answer the school phone? How long must a parent or student spend waiting for someone to look up when standing in the school office?

How long must a teacher wait before receiving needed supplies or a chance to use the phone? How long must a teacher wait before copies are returned from the Xerox machine?

In a free market, choice-driven school system, these behaviors would change. Perhaps we will see the introduction of "fast schools" and "fast learning." Renzulli and his colleagues (1983) suggest a learning strategy called "curriculum compacting." (Someone must have watched what happens to trash and decided that some of the ditto pages, workbook exercises and other busy work deserve equal treatment.) They suggest assigning only as much practice as an individual student needs to achieve mastery. Assessment prior to instruction relieves students from unnecessary drudgery. Many can then move swiftly on to other learning opportunities.

Not everything that is good and worthwhile can or should be done swiftly, but many things should be dispensed with rapidly. We would be wise to examine all existing practices with time in mind.

Some would have us add more time to the school day and the school year in order to compete with the Japanese. Would it not make more sense to make better use of the time we have now so that learning might flourish within existing resources? Is more bad wine a good substitute for careful aging and distilling?

11

WHAT DOES **CONVENIENCE** HAVE TO DO WITH SCHOOLS?

Tucker demonstrates how convenience is often the deciding factor when a consumer makes a market choice. The basic product of two companies may be essentially the same, but various convenience factors can separate them in the minds of the consumer. To what extent does the company make it easy to pay for or order the product? What are its hours of operation? Does the consumer have to miss a day's work in order to be on hand for delivery?

Schools often seem to organize such activities as parent conferences as if convenience was not a factor at all. It is not unusual to send home a letter announcing that the parent's conference is scheduled for 10:00 a.m. on a weekday morning without ever asking the parent what is convenient.

In a similar fashion, little thought is given to the inconvenience teachers must suffer in contacting the outside world, either to speak with parents about school matters or to conduct personal business. Phones are few and far between. Phones offering confidentiality are even harder to come by.

Some schools now put phones in teachers' rooms. Others provide portable phones that can be borrowed during prep periods. In an Age of Information, it is understood in these schools that professional performance and morale require convenient and confidential communications systems.

How convenient is it for a student to meet with a teacher to get help? How convenient is it for a teacher to meet with a colleague to conduct peer coaching? College professors have ample time for convenient access to each other and to students, but teachers of younger students have no such convenience.

WHAT DO **AGE WAVES** HAVE TO DO WITH SCHOOLS?

Tucker points out that the population breaks down into three main waves: the mature market, the baby boom, and the baby bust. Each has its own preferences. Each requires special attention.

Take a look at school elections. In most towns a mere 8 to 10% of the population bothers to vote. In many cases, the budget decision becomes a contest between two factions: the mature market (senior citizens) versus the baby boom (parents). If Tucker is correct that the over-65 group is the fastest growing segment of the population, what are the implications for schools?

What do schools do to redefine their services to satisfy all three waves? If the mature market is helping to pay the bills, what have we been doing for them to make them feel they are getting their money's worth?

During a decade when our client base may shrink in relation to the population as a whole, we might be wise to redefine that client base, and to offer a broader array of services to a broader age spectrum.

In some districts there is a heavy commitment to community service. Students help seniors with snow-covered walks, provide shopping services, and offer company for shut-ins. In other districts, seniors are encouraged to make use of such school facilities as desktop publishing equipment, which helps them reach their fellows through newsletters, or dining facilities, which provide healthy food and companionship.

WHAT DOES CHOICE HAVE TO DO WITH SCHOOLS?

We serve a public that is coming to expect that it will get what it wants in the form that it wants it. In the marketplace, the companies that customize most successfully win the greatest market share.

The typical public school still operates under mass-marketing principles. The main concession to market segmenting is tracking, offering different educational products to different groups. In many places, little effort is expended on understanding the customers and little value is placed on their preferences.

Even in classrooms themselves there is a remarkable sameness of instruction, which has been well-documented by such observers as Goodlad (1984) and Sizer (1984). Classrooms offer little room for student questions and curiosity. National studies report a preponderance of teacher questions, almost to the exclusion of student questions, with a ratio of 38 teacher questions for every 1 student question (Hyman, 1980). Students travel down a learning path determined by the teacher and the textbook publishers. They have little choice and little opportunity to make their own meaning.

In trying to make all their publics happy, many schools rely on the least common denominator. They round off the edges, eliminate the controversial, and produce what is too often a bland form of learning. Contributing to this phenomenon are state testing initiatives, which act to enforce standardization. Ironically, even many of the proponents of "school choice" have insisted on a national test!

Schools will have to deal with the issue of choice. And they must see that choice can be healthy. For example, in Buffalo, New York, where choice was actually a desegregation strategy, every school became a magnet school, each with a special mission and flavor. Speak with staff members, and they will tell you that their school is the best in the city. When the staff and the clients are in a school because they choose to be there and happen to believe in the principles associated with that school, there is a remarkable sense of purpose and passion often missing in the schools that seek mass appeal.

If the public schools do not provide their clients with choice, others will take the initiative. Many proponents of choice want to throw all schools into an open market and to provide parents with vouchers. They seem insensitive to arguments against segmenting the American population by color, creed, national origin, or gender. They place little value on public schools as instruments of nation-building. If these powerful people reach their goal, we will see a dramatic shift in how education is provided and defined.

Those school systems that move today to listen to client needs and interests may learn enough about customizing learning to hold on to their market share. But those who leave their heads planted firmly in the sand may be in serious trouble at the end of the decade.

What does LIFESTYLE have to do with schools?

Tucker points out that major shifts in the way people spend their lives can have disastrous effects upon companies that are not alert and responsive to those changes. For example, as many families shifted so that both parents worked full time, such activities as sewing decreased. This change in lifestyle seriously affected the sewing-machine market.

In schools, we have seen changes in lifestyle dramatically alter the nature of childhood. The family dinner time seems a relic, as each person eats a microwave dinner in a separate room in front of a different TV screen. Communication between parents and children has diminished. Many children go home to empty houses. Institutions such as families and churches, which once played a major role in teaching children values, seem to have much less influence than previously. Attitudes toward authority, which broke down during the Vietnam era, have undermined the traditional respect paid to teachers. Children often are dropped off an hour before school to wait in freezing weather for the doors to open. Many children either make their own breakfast or skip it.

In many cities and suburbs, teenage students have become heavy workers outside of the school day, bankrolling extravagant lifestyles and wardrobes with earnings from retail and fast-food jobs that keep them from their school work and leave them sleepy when they show up for school each day. The business world, which is so quick to cast blame on the schools for poor performance, is quick to engage in such child labor, even though it has serious negative consequences for the long-term health of the nation.

As lifestyle changes swirl around us, the nature of childhood and learning itself shifts. Proponents of "schooling the way it used to be" argue for more hours of homework, as if the American home were still the residence of Ozzie and Harriet. We are competing as educators with home-schooling in the form of TV and with employers who play to our students' materialistic desires. TV creates the desires. Employers seduce students into evening employment. Learning comes last.

What can we do? Join the local Chamber of Commerce and educate business to its responsibilities. Work with political leaders to review state laws regarding child labor. Are the laws passed at the turn of the century still valid and appropriate? What changes are needed?

Those schools that limit their definition of responsibility to classroom instruction between 9:00 and 3:00 may fail this generation of children. Those that reach out to bring the community into the schools, that work actively on community-building and development—for example, with Comer's successful projects (1992) in New Haven—are shifting their mission to match the needs of their charges.

WHAT DOES **DISCOUNTING** HAVE TO DO WITH SCHOOLS?

Some companies gain an early advantage in an industry that permits them to charge a premium for their product or service without worrying about competition. After years of surging along making big profits with little competition, such companies often grow fat and lazy, rather than lean and fit.

16

They grow used to doing business with a bloated payroll and organization.

Along comes a newcomer with a lean and hungry look, determined to offer the same product or service at a vast discount, cutting out all frills and extras in order to offer a significantly lower price. The older company usually sneers and dismisses the potential threat, assuming that customers will remain loyal to the industry leader. The field is littered with the casualties of such arrogance, as customers flock by the millions to the newcomer. Even after reality sets in, the old company cannot even begin to understand how the rules of the game have changed, cannot begin to restructure radically enough to meet the new competition on equal terms. In many cases, bankruptcy is the only fate.

Whittle (Olson, 1992) already has mentioned discounting in his description of the new schools he will be launching. He intends to approach school boards in poorly achieving urban districts and offer to educate students in his schools for significantly less per student than the board is capable of doing. Will they give it a try? What do they have to lose? What do they have to gain? Did *Channel One* fly?

If you are starting new schools from scratch, think of the economic advantages. You can avoid featherbedding and hire the most-qualified teachers. You need not pay people based on seniority. Are the dollars currently spent paying people for years of service and numbers of graduate credits related to quality? Could one buy better quality for less money? That remains to be seen; but it is clear that a free-market approach to education may bring with it serious discounting, which may leave the old "education companies" staggering.

WHAT DOES VALUE-ADDING, HAVE TO DO WITH SCHOOLS?

Anyone who has spent time in hotels during the past decade has enjoyed the fruits of an expanding commitment to such "extras" as free toiletries and frequent traveller clubs, which are intended to develop loyalty and appreciation. Just as the wise company attends to adding value to basic products or services, schools might ask how they might add value to the basics of schooling.

Instead of handing out free shampoo or a morning newspaper, a school might go for items of greater value, giving each student the ability to reason or work out surprising problems with independence and ingenuity. To enhance the value of this gift, the school might endorse each student's diploma with a guarantee stipulating the advanced competencies possessed by that student, so that a potential employer or college might know what kind of person is knocking on their door.

Value adding, in yet another sense, might refer to the community citizens, who pay for schools through taxation but may feel they receive little in return. The wise school keeps its doors open well beyond the "normal" school day and provides a wide range of services to this broader community. Some schools send students out into the community to provide services, a human return on investment. Thus the community comes to see the school as a valued partner.

In yet another sense, a well-respected, effective school system drives up the value of real estate, because parents search for the best education they can afford. Affluent parents, in particular, have been exercising choice in their home-buying behaviors for many years. Value-adding comes into this equation by virtue of a system's skill at advertising the fact of its excellence.

What does CUSTOMER SERVICE have to do with schools?

All too many schools take their clients (parents and students) for granted. It is almost as if they have forgotten why they exist. In an open market, this attitude would lead to extinction; clients would flee to other service providers who cater to their interests, needs, and preferences. In fact, school systems in affluent communities often find themselves in competition with private schools, which are trying to lure away their clients with much better treatment.

Frustrated with the benign neglect typical of their child's last public school, parents moving cross-country call up the local high school in the town where they might live and find themselves speaking with the principal, who has been called to the phone by an enthusiastic secretary. The head of the school speaks with great enthusiasm about the school and asks a dozen or more questions about the child, seeming genuinely interested in meeting her. The phone conversation ends with an appointment for a guided tour and a session with a guidance counselor, who will, they are assured, tailor a program to meet their daughter's needs. "Let me send you a video our students made about the school and two brochures describing our programs and where our students go on to college."

The secret to effective customer service is to find out what customers really care about and then to set up a strategy to make sure they receive what they desire, as long as it is consistent with sound educational philosophy. Davidow and Uttal (1989) offer a six-point plan that outlines how to build a great customer service program:

- Devise a service strategy
- Get top managers to act like service fanatics
- Concentrate on motivating and training employees
- Design products and services that make good customer service possible
- Invest in service infrastructure
- Monitor achievement of customer service goals

While a school will need to adjust these suggestions and strategies to fit an educational context, their book offers a good starting point for a group to begin the customer-service planning process.

What does TECHNO-EDGE have to do with schools?

While automatic tellers have revolutionized the once-conservative banking industry, schools have been very slow to embrace new technologies in ways that might improve student performance, customer service, or school effectiveness. It is not due to lack of investment; rather, it is due to a lack of *systemic* investment. In far too many cases, new technologies are purchased without posing the systemic questions that deserve consideration. "What should we do with this equipment?" is too often asked after the equipment has been bought.

School planners might divide technology questions into two categories:

1) In what powerful ways might new technologies change our system for organizing and providing learning experiences in concert with district goals?

2) In what powerful ways might new technologies change our system for delivering information and service to staff, to parents, and to students?

The key word in each is "system."

Because much of this book is devoted to considering such questions, it requires little space here; one example will suffice for now. Ameritech's *Project Homeroom* has electronically linked students, parents, and teachers in a group of Chicago-area high schools by providing them with home computers, modems, and *Prodigy*™. The isolation and fragmentation characteristic of the old communication system is replaced by connectedness. Parents are no longer frozen out of the action, and their information needs can now be met swiftly and efficiently.

As parents become accustomed to an array of products that reflect the national preoccupation with quality, it will not be long before they begin requiring the same from their schools. It will no longer suffice to judge schools by the number of students who "pass through" to graduate. It will no longer suffice to judge them by their standardized test scores or college entrance results. The clients will rightly ask, "But what value did you add to this child I sent to you? What competencies did you give her or him? What can they do now that they could not do before? And how efficiently and effectively did you accomplish this task?"

Unfortunately, Sizer (1984) and Goodlad (1984) both portray a dismal process of moving students through school in a credentialing process that has more to do with the collection of credits and hours than it does with learning.

A commitment to quality will require a dramatic shift in the culture and purpose of schools. All employees must ask daily how their performance can be changed to enhance quality. All systems must be under constant review and critique. Coverage of curriculum and a focus on credits must be replaced with an emphasis on the process of learning, instructional strategies, and clearly defined student outcomes. Teachers must be given time to work in teams and act experimentally to change existing systems. Resources must be provided to support ongoing adult learning. Outmoded traditions and practices such as tracking—which act to define and limit student "potentials"—must be replaced with new systems that challenge all students to exceed the expectations we once might have imposed.

PART FOUR:
FUTURE PERFECT PLANNING

Much of the current talk about restructuring schools and national goals may be seriously flawed by the planning models urged on school leaders by their erstwhile corporate "friends." Unfortunately, traditional strategic planning, which has served many companies poorly in coping with turbulence and discontinuous change (IBM and Sears, for example), remains the tool of choice for many districts planning their voyage of change.

Future Perfect by Stanley M. Davis (1987), which Tom Peters calls the "book of the decade," offers a vastly different approach to planning, one that frees us from the anchors of the past, the blinders that block innovative thinking.

Davis sees traditional planning as seriously limited because it "relies too heavily upon environmental scanning and existing paradigms." He goes on to say that "if strategy is the codification of what has already taken place, then it is the enemy of innovation" (p. 27). Traditional planning does not address discontinuous change.

Discontinuous change represents major upheavals and transformations that change basic rules and structures. A prime example is the recent change in the USSR, which went from world power to world beggar in a single year.

The trouble with traditional planning is its reliance on projections. Once a trend appears, traditional planning tends to assume that it will run its course. In times of turbulence, it is likely that some trends will evaporate or reverse, only to be replaced by new ones that no one predicted. In such times, we must be skilled at thinking the unthinkable, because it is likely to occur.

Visions of the future formed out of a traditional planning base are not likely to exploit fully the potential of the future, because the past will weigh too heavily upon the thinking of the group. What has been and what has failed in the past will serve to keep dreams and visions suppressed. The old paradigms will shape the thinking and the planning.

For a school district, future perfect planning might mean that a team of planners, parents, teachers, students, administrators, board members, business people, professors and community members should devote a year or two to deciding what learning might be like in the year 2005: What should be the kinds of experiences and outcomes available? How should it feel to be a learner? What might the environment be? How would one spend a day? Once the group has reached consensus on what the future should be, they turn their attention back to the present. However, they look back to the present from the perspective of the future, from the year 2005, as if they are in that future condition and they ask, "How will they (the people in 1993) get here (the year 2005)?"

As Davis explains it, "The only way an organization's leaders can get there (the objectives of the strategy) from here (the current organization) is to lead from a place in time that assumes you are already there, and that is determined even though it hasn't happened yet" (p. 25). "Organizations that foster innovation are not to be wedded to strategy as formal planning, but to strategy as intuition" (p. 27).

The path from 1993 to 2005 is much more open to imaginative thinking when viewed from the future perfect perspective Davis advocates. A team is less likely to create a four-inch-thick, long-range plan to guide the district through the next decade because it will be apparent that forward movement will require much experimentation and invention, that it will necessitate steering rather than operating on auto-pilot. Planning is not something that occurs once every 5 to 10 years. It is an ongoing, developmental process closely associated with learning.

Twenty years of so-called educational reform have shown little in the way of results because we persist with measurement and strategies better suited for a smokestack society than an Age of Information. If we wish change to be more than

23

an academic exercise in futility, we must throw off our anchors and try some real sailing.

PART FIVE:
MICHAEL FULLAN'S IMPLEMENTATION DIP

One of the most illuminating works on educational change is Michael Fullan's *The New Meaning of Educational Change* (1991). Fullan has identified an "implementation dip" that seems to greet almost any school innovation. The implementation dip is a period of time during which high expectations are disappointed by the onset of discomforting realities. It seems that innovations too often are accompanied with large promises, yet the morning after often leaves us disillusioned and hung-over.

In reviewing site-based management projects from around the country, one finds considerable evidence of Fullan's implementation dip. High hopes often are followed by months of negotiation and discussion, with relatively little change for students and teachers in classrooms. In many articles, the leaders warn others to prepare participants more carefully for the change experience, so that disillusionment will not be such a strong factor.

PART SIX:
WHATEVER HAPPENED TO LEADERSHIP?

There is some evidence that the society has grown wary of leaders and leadership. After a few brief years of speaking of the principal as instructional leader, we suddenly are thrust into a preference for group decision-making.

While there is some evidence that collaborative group process might be one of the best ways to develop group commitment to innovation, there also is considerable evidence that groups without the prerequisite collaborative culture and process skills can waste many hours and months in combat, gridlock, and "group think," which does little good for students or teachers (McKenzie, 1991). We must not be naive about the prospects for instructional change which accompany a change in organizational structure. Some teachers will welcome the opportunity to forge ahead into new frontiers, while others may take advantage of new power and influence to settle old scores. The same can be said for principals and parents. It may prove to be the best of worlds or the very worst.

Those who work as leaders in school districts probably have learned first-hand of this tendency to distrust leaders. Few would consider launching a major new initiative without very carefully cultivating the soil far in advance of planting any seeds. Unlike the entrepreneurs lauded by management guru Peter Drucker (1985), school leaders are forced to devote months to persuasion and argument before launching any real activity. True experimentation rarely is permitted, because everybody demands certainty: "How do we know this is going to work?"

Leadership in schools during this decade will increasingly require indirection and subtlety, persuasion and coalition building, consensus and partnership. Insight will not suffice. Boldness may be little valued—that is, unless we are forced into a free market where the Whittles of the world will use boldness to drive traditional schools out of business, discounting their educational products, exploiting lifestyle changes, and providing customer service that makes older schools appear insensitive.

What price change? The answer will depend on the stance we take and the rules we must follow. In times as turbulent as these, we must remember the wisdom of Will Rogers:

"Even if you're on the right track, you'll get run over if you just sit there."

CHAPTER TWO

ENGENDERING A CHANGE ETHIC
IN THE NEXT GENERATION

Although almost everyone concedes that the next century will be characterized by startling change, shifting rules, and persistent uncertainty, we continue to educate children as if this were the 1950s, as if they could look forward to a life of tranquility and predictability. We should remember that as soon as former President Bush announced the end of the Cold War, we found ourselves in the largest military mobilization since Vietnam. The collapse of the USSR, instead of translating into immediate security, led to dangerous regional instability and ethnic combat. American schools must prepare a generation to embrace change with enthusiasm, to welcome surprise, and to thrive on chaos. It is our duty to create citizens with a change ethic.

In *Managing as a Performing Art*, Peter Vaill (1989) portrays life in the Information Age as "permanent white water." One can never be quite sure what lies around the bend of the river . . . a stretch of calm or a thunderous waterfall.

After decades of teaching students to color between the lines, obey the rules and avoid rocking the boat, we now must recognize that these behaviors are a sure recipe for extinction, an archaic collection of dinosaur strategies that inhibit adapta-

27

tion, stifle inventiveness and undermine competitiveness. To cope with rapidly shifting contexts, we need citizens and employees who are quick on their feet . . . people who are willing to rock the boat, make waves, and ask questions. We need employees and citizens with a *change ethic*.

How do we raise a generation with a change ethic? We make change and surprise constant elements in our classrooms. We attack routine and humdrum with adventure, inquiry, and investigation. We ask students to wrestle with essential questions that awaken curiosity and provoke learning. We invite students to make meaning out of chaos and nonsense. We replace the ho-hum routines of Industrial Age textbooks, ditto sheets, and fill-in-the-blanks learning with problems, challenges, and issues drawn from the "real world." We open up schools so that the world is the classroom instead of the classroom being the world. We create a change ethic by offering students a "real time" education in "real time" schools.

"But this will be costly!" some critics complain. However, it will be costlier not to do so. A nation that can afford to bail out savings and loan institutions to the tune of hundreds of billions of dollars can ill afford to mortgage its future by neglecting its young.

If civic virtue is an insufficient argument for strong schools, enlightened self-interest should win the day, as critics see their retirement threatened by the prospect of a weak economy and an unskilled workforce. Before long, there will be only 2 to 3 workers for each recipient of Social Security, far fewer workers per recipient than there were a decade ago. If the retirees of the future are to rest easy, the future workers must be able to cope with change.

CHAPTER THREE

HYPER-NAVIGATING:
BASIC SKILL OR THE NEW SHOW-AND-TELL?

How many school districts have listed *hyper-navigating* as a basic skill to be acquired by students prior to graduation? How prominently have they identified multimedia skills in their agenda for 21st century preparation? How much attention is devoted to developing visual literacy so that these future citizens can critically evaluate the visual information bombarding them?

According to Toffler (1990), power now flows to those with the skill to transform data into information and insight. (Throughout this book, the word "insight" will be substituted for "knowledge" when referring to this concept, because it connotes a higher level of understanding.) The war against Iraq confirmed this phenomenon, as information technologies played a critical role in the conquest of Iraq's "smokestack" army by our own high-tech, "smart" forces and weapons.

Toffler suggests that civilization is moving from force and money to knowledge as the key to power. Influence will go to those who are skilled at converting data—seemingly disconnected fragments—into information and then insight. This process requires pattern identification. The observer or analyst must know how to identify relationships and connections,

29

transforming the swirl of data into trends, cause-and-effect associations, and general laws or principles.

Reich (1991) claims that our workforce has split into two main groups: service workers and "symbolic analysts." The nation's bounty flows generously to the second group. Reich notes that these workers are especially skilled at solving, identifying, and brokering problems by manipulating symbols—words, numbers, or visual images (pp. 177-79). He points out that this kind of thinking is in high demand by a world economy that stresses problem identification and problem solving.

Where does *hyper-navigating* fit into all of this? Mary Alice White of Teachers College (1984) argues that although we receive more than half of our information about the world visually, schools have done little to formalize a curriculum commitment to the development of visual literacy. According to White, little time is devoted to teaching students how to interpret visual data with critical analysis. Even less time is spent on teaching students to make use of these visual data to communicate messages.

Hyper-navigating is multi-dimensional, requiring students to pass through several sequences and levels of exploration and reporting:

1) Students should be able to find their way purposefully through oceans of numerical, text-based, and visual information with various software tools—such as Optical Data's *Videocards*™, ABC News Interactive's *HyperCard*™ program, or Voyager *Videostack*™—seeking answers to what Ted Sizer would call "essential questions."

2) Students should be able to peer past the details and facts of pictures, diagrams, charts, tables, and graphs to discern meaning. They should be able to "harvest" these data; scan and browse thoughtfully; seek patterns, rela-

tionships, anomalies, and significance; and be able to find those data that help to clarify issues, resolve problems, or suggest solutions.

3) Students should be able to convert the data into information and insight, translating them into new formats —such as pictures, graphs, or videodisc presentations— so they can demonstrate and share insights.

4) Students should be able to employ a variety of desktop presentation, video, and multimedia programs to share their findings coherently, comprehensively, and persuasively to show that they can synthesize the data and convert information and knowledge into insight.

The good hyper-navigator can penetrate the fog, the confusion, the distortion, the mountains of data and the propaganda of modern life to catch and transmit an elucidating glimpse of reality.

Advertisers and promoters may not welcome such critical analysis. For a country that selects presidents and governors on the basis of sound bites and carefully orchestrated media events, critical analysis could be unsettling. Can a consumer society thrive if the consumers begin to ask thoughtful questions about visual messages and information technologies? Would people continue to use their bank cards to buy groceries if they knew how the data is being compiled, stored, and used?

Techno-savvy schools forge ahead and create the kinds of multimedia and desktop video experiences that make hyper-navigating an everyday event. What are you and your school district doing to incorporate hyper-navigating and visual literacy into your curriculum?

CHAPTER FOUR

THE PUZZLING TASK OF RESTRUCTURING SCHOOLS

The task of restructuring schools is much like working on a jigsaw puzzle made up of dozens of ill-matching pieces. Old paradigms act like glue, keeping us from "unsticking" past practice. Restructuring requires synthesis—rearrangement of the ingredients or school puzzle pieces listed below. Note how frequently change efforts neglect one or more of these elements:

Tests	Curriculum
Texts	Instructional Techniques
Staff Development	Money
Technologies	Research
Program Evaluation	Leadership
Technical Assistance	Change Strategies
Political Support	Needs Assessment
Innovative Ideas	Time
Faith	Motivation
Facilities	Staff
Real World Data	Planning
Organizational Culture	Tradition
Policy	Instructional Practices
Relationships	Students
Parents	Community

How do these pieces all fit together to make sense? How might we alter or rearrange the pieces and their relationship to each other? Does your change effort address all of these pieces?

BREAKING PARADIGM PARALYSIS

A paradigm is a way of thinking, perceiving, and acting that has become fully ingrained in the life of an organization. Paradigm paralysis is a condition of blindness to changing conditions that require new ways of thinking, perceiving, and acting; it blocks responsible adaptation.

SMOKESTACK PARADIGM	INFORMATION AGE PARADIGM
Some children can learn and some children can learn to reason.	All children can learn and all children can learn to reason.
The job of schools is to teach children compliance and facts.	The job of schools is to teach children problem-solving and reasoning.
The job of schools is to teach memorization of scripts.	The job of schools is to teach scripts and script-writing.
Practice makes perfect and the more the better.	Script repair must accompany remediation.
Remediation is perennial.	Remediation is temporary.
The teacher provides the insight and the student commits to memory.	The student creates insight and the teacher provides guidance.
Technology as teacher.	Technology as tool.

The journey of change will involve schools in laying aside the archaic mindsets of the past in favor of new, Information Age paradigms like those above.

CHAPTER FIVE

DISARMING THE CYCLOPS: USING *CHANNEL ONE* TO TEACH VISUAL LITERACY

If a school district accepts the offer of "free" TV monitors, which Whittle Communications uses to pry classroom doors open to *Channel One*'s daily news programs and advertising, teachers and administrators at least can convert these commercials into powerful educational lessons that might increase children's resistance to advertising and propaganda.

If we must face the Cyclops in our classrooms each day, we can seize the opportunity to raise a generation of savvy consumers with visual literacy skills—the ability to think critically and powerfully about visual information and media.

Why not turn *Channel One* around and use it to teach critical analysis of advertising techniques? Daily, thoughtful critiques of commercial messages by all teachers and students in a carefully orchestrated program of media education could pay great dividends. Students would learn to probe beyond the surface meanings of news programs and advertising to see how truth can be distorted or persuasion might cross the line into propaganda.

Exposing school children to even more television advertising by allowing *Channel One* into the nation's classrooms is hard to defend. However, Toffler (1991) suggests that one of our primary goals is to prepare this generation to resist the "Info-Tactics" of powerful interest groups, who will twist information to serve their own ends, subverting democratic society by manipulating its citizens.

As a superintendent, I strongly opposed the invasion of schools by commercial messages. I still argue against giving *Channel One* the time with a captive student audience. But for those who must "look the Cyclops in the eye" each day, there is a powerful way to convert the intruder into a useful guest. Teachers and administrators in such districts should arm themselves with critical-viewing packages, which convert the daily commercials and news programs into a wholesome experience for citizenship and consumer education.

Schools that fail to provide ongoing experience with critical analysis of TV advertising and news are failing to do their job. They are inadequately preparing young people for citizenship in a society where information is communicated through predominantly visual media. In a society that markets presidential candidates with sound bites and careful packaging, citizenship education must necessarily take young people past the surface symbols and teach them how to evaluate the candidates on the basis of their track records and positions on the issues. We must help them to understand that whether a candidate is seen driving a tank or waving a flag has little to do with questions of competence.

Some teachers claim that students pay little attention to *Channel One* or to its accompanying advertising, that they tune it all out. These reports of passive TV viewing are of little comfort. Claims that advertising goes unnoticed conflict with evidence that ad campaigns create enough sales to justify the millions of dollars they cost. Advertisers want entrance to schools because they know that their ads will communicate effectively and powerfully. If you have any doubt, look at student footwear or ask about acne creams.

Commercial messages are usually emotional rather than rational. Often, the messages are imbedded in subliminal content—non-verbal messages that seek out the child's core feelings. If we convert the pictures into words they would tell us:

"Buy our deodorant so you won't be embarrassed."

"Buy our mouth spray so you won't lose your friends."

"Buy our hair spray so you won't be alone Saturday night."

"Buy *Brand X* because that's what cool people buy."

Barring parental or school intervention, these commercial messages threaten to undermine the basis for student decision-making skills before they are ever established. They attempt to program children to equate well-being with the possession of certain products. Self-worth is defined by what kind of car one drives, what kind of house one occupies, and what kind of beer one drinks.

Years of advertising teach the child:

"Say Yes to our deodorant."

"Say Yes to our mouth spray."

"Say Yes to our beer."

"Say Yes to our sleeping pills."

"Say Yes to our candidate."

And then well-meaning folks try to turn it all around with a much weaker, poorly financed campaign to teach the adolescent to say "NO" to drugs.

Unfortunately, with the advent of the Information Age and multimedia's powerful tools, the bombardment is likely to grow more intense, more subtle, more persuasive, and more pervasive during the next decade. Computers and marketing experts have combined forces to develop potent campaigns designed to persuade us to choose products and candidates without regard to quality, value, or track record. These campaigns increasingly rely on appeals to fears, base emotions, and anxieties, rather than reason.

There certainly are better ways to teach visual literacy than allowing *Channel One* into our schools. Using videotapes and videodiscs, schools can provide students with a limited and carefully selected diet of visual messages for critical analysis. The point is that visual literacy is too important to leave to chance.

Working as a consultant on multimedia with teachers across the country, I have found that videodiscs, such as ABC News Interactive's *Vote '88,* teach powerful lessons about advertising and politics. Students can slow down sound bites from 30 frames per second to one frame every three seconds. At this slower speed, one can note the racial composition of both Bush and Dukakis ads on prison furlough programs and ask what impact was intended.

Using videodiscs, one can freeze frames to examine background content and staging. One can turn off the narrator's voice to focus on visual content. Such careful analysis in a social studies program can go a long way toward developing the kinds of critical viewers our democracy deserves, and it can do so without subjecting students to daily commercials touting the advantages of various acne creams. Such experiences should be blended throughout a district's K-12 curriculum scope and sequence in social studies, language arts, and the sciences. This approach to media saves valuable instructional time while addressing critically important citizenship skills. It disarms the Cyclops.

Chapter Six

TELECOMMUNICATIONS, SCHOOLS, AND THE GLOBAL VILLAGE

The world is the classroom.

The classroom is not the world.

New technologies may open windows to the world.

—J. A. McKenzie

The Need for Everyday Heroes and Brainworkers

The primary challenge of schools in this decade is the development of a generation of thinkers and "everyday heroes" (Catford and Ray, 1991), that is, young people capable of gaining insight from confusing data and then taking action to improve the society. Toffler (1991) and others have demonstrated that this global information-driven economy requires inventive, problem-solving "brainworkers" at all levels—even at the customer service desk where pay may be only $6.00 an hour.

As rapid response to changing conditions becomes the basis for competitive advantage in an information-driven society, the workplace demands innovation, quick thinking, flexibility, and empathy from front-line workers, as well as from managers. The best workers, citizens, and family members will be able to make up their own minds. They will be highly skilled at juggling fragments, cues, and clues in order to puzzle out their own meanings.

New technologies can provide the tools, the workbench, and the laboratory students need for the development of such information skills.

THE NEED FOR SCRIPT WRITERS

The days are over when we can rely on memorization of scripts and other people's insights. Smokestack schools long have emphasized the teaching of basic patterns of problems and their solutions, so that students know what to do when facing certain predictable tests and word problems. These basic patterns, "mental scripts," work only as long as the problems match the patterns stored in one's memory. Information Age schools must go beyond mere memorization of scripts to teach students "script writing," the actual invention of new approaches to unfamiliar problems.

Take the following problem, for example:

> *There was a group of 5 shelters built alongside the water. Men, women, and children lived in the shelters. In the water there were five boats, anchored and waiting. Each morning 10 men and 6 women climbed into rowboats. Then they climbed into two fishing boats. They carried 16 sacks with them. The sacks were dripping and moving. They dropped the sacks in the bottom of their boats. One boat lifted sails and headed out to sea. When the sun began to drop, four men and 2 women headed back to land. This time there were more than 30 sacks dripping. Seventeen children came out to meet them. It was midnight before the other boat paddled back to shore. Their sacks were empty.*

What would your students do with this paragraph if you presented it as a problem? Because it does not have a clear question attached to it, it breaks the rules (script) right from the start. As with real life, the problem must be found. The student must sort through the fragments and use questions to determine what to do with the data. The student is challenged to invent a problem or question. This thought process is more analogous to adult problem-solving than are the patterned (scripted) patterns one encounters in many texts. Try it out and see what they do with it.

How about this one? It is a many-step word problem:

Mary's allowance is $ 3.75 weekly. She has managed to save the following amounts for the last few months:

Jan 1	$2.75
Jan 8	$3.25
Jan 15	$3.00
Jan 22	$1.45
Jan 29	$1.97
Feb 5	$3.06
Feb 12	$3.20
Feb 19	$2.90
Feb 26	$2.37

Mary goes on a shopping trip with her savings and stops at a half-dozen stores, making a number of purchases. She buys lipstick at one store for $2.79. She buys 4 pairs of socks at another store, which is selling 2 pairs for $7.00. She buys a magazine for $2.25 and three pencils for $.28 each. Can she still afford to pay $4.00 for a matinee and buy an ice cream sundae with her friend if one sundae costs $ 1.75? If no, how much more will she need? If yes, how much change will she have? Given her past savings record, how many weeks *would it take for Mary to save enough for a $28.00 cassette player?*

The solution to this problem requires some invention. Polya's work (1963) on "heuristics" suggests the strategy of "chunking," breaking down big problems into small ones (analysis) and then rearranging the parts (synthesis) to create an answer.

In a similar fashion, those of us who have struggled to teach inference to young people know that "reading between the lines" requires script writing. If the main idea of a paragraph is not clearly stated, many students flounder, even if provided with four choices. See if your students can fashion main ideas to go with each of the following:

NUMBER ONE (PRIMARY GRADES)

It is dirty. The food tastes bad. They have no toys. There is no playground. It costs too much. The seats hurt. It is noisy.

NUMBER TWO (LATE ELEMENTARY)

They have not won a game in weeks. Morale is low. He has made some bad strategic decisions. The owners are angry. Gate receipts are down. The TV station is threatening to cancel its contract. The state is considering throwing the team out of the stadium. We are headed for the bottom of the league.

Here they really must write scripts, make their own meaning, convert data into insight. How much practice do students require with this sort of puzzling and script writing? What is a reasonable investment of school time in such thinking activities?

THE NEED FOR FUNDAMENTAL RESTRUCTURING OF SCHOOLING

Educators need the time, the resources, and the permission to re-invent the meaning of schooling—time to work together to build new programs and to dismantle the mind-numbing hardware of the Industrial Age. If schools are to stress puzzling and the learning of script-writing, they must be restructured. What is meant by "restructuring"? Mojkowski and Bamberger (1991) offer the following definitions:

Restructuring is the process of institutionalizing new beliefs and values in the school mission, structure, and process. The gaps between these new essentials and the existing missions, structures, and processes signal the level and type of changes needed (p. 9).

Restructuring schools often make substantial adjustments in instructional practices, often redesigning the entire teaching and learning process and environment. In these schools, teachers:

- *infuse real-world learning and work into their instruction and place more responsibility on students to work both independently and collaboratively.*

- *use time and other resources differently to create and sustain these environments.*

- *provide equal and extended opportunity and access to all of the school's learning resources.*

- *design instructional alternatives to accommodate the range of abilities and talents; and*

- *reorganize instruction so that students truly understand the material presented to them (as well as the knowledge they create themselves), experience more in-depth learning as opposed to covering great amounts of content, and engage in higher-order thinking and learning tasks (pp. 10-11).*

Schools engaged in restructuring employ integrated top-down and bottom-up approaches to change. Organizational structures are based on networks and flexible work groups rather than on hierarchies (p. 11).

43

These schools catalyze and support new roles for teachers. They encourage risk-taking and innovation. In the classroom, teachers serve as instructional designers, coaches, resources, and facilitators. Outside of the classroom, they serve as members of teams working on improvement projects agreed on by the staff (p. 13).

The Need for Less formal Instructional Time

Despite all the talk about extending the school year and day, our students should actually spend less time in rows of desks in classrooms absorbing teacher wisdom and insights.

Imagine the wonders we could do if formal classroom contact was reduced to 15 to 20 hours per week, with students enjoying far more opportunities for active learning, research, and exploration. While they explore, the professionals might plan, invent, learn new skills, and consult, building great new places for learning to occur. They might work with students in small groups and tutorials. They might visit the workplaces of, and form teams and partnerships with, business people, scientists, farmers, and a host of interesting resource people.

Talk about a major paradigm shift! "Less is more," (Sizer, 1992) relates to the structure of school systems as much as it does to the curriculum. If we are bogged down in "activity traps," like covering too many facts in too little time or meeting with children to the exclusion of professional dialogue and learning, we stand little chance of meeting the society's need for a vibrant educational response to change.

We might use the Renzulli "curriculum compacting" strategy (1983) to drastically reduce the mindless busywork and unnecessary practice at low levels of *Bloom's Taxonomy* (1954), which according to studies by Goodlad (1984), Sizer (1984), and others, currently characterize far too much of the time spent in American classrooms.

44

For example, take the typical fourth grade math program. What does the textbook require from students during the first four months of school? Review. Why? We are told students are supposed to forget the previous year's skills during the summer. As an elementary principal, this practice used to bother me, because I personally knew that many of the students had not forgotten the skills and were actually ready to move along on new material in September.

I asked the staff to test every student during the first week of school in order to figure out which students needed the review. We found that less than half needed the review. The others raced forward, gaining an extra four months of instruction that year and each of the following three years in that school. We added 40% to the school year without changing the schedule. Test scores soared. Student and teacher pride soared.

In the same way, high school teachers usually blame long lists of biological facts for keeping them and their students out of the streams and natural environments where they might do real exploration and experimentation. We need to re-examine the time-honored practices of smokestack education and replace them with new paradigms that make students the real learners, inventors, discoverers, and seekers for truth.

Are we keeping students sitting in classrooms in rows doing ditto sheets (often 10 or more daily) because we know it enhances learning? Is the lecture really the best way to prepare students for active and independent problem-solving as citizens of the Information Age? Does learning actually improve by spending more time at smokestack tasks?

THE POTENTIAL OF NEW TECHNOLOGIES TO OPEN THE WINDOW

New technologies can support radically different conceptions of schooling and learning, if we will but challenge some of the basic assumptions that block us from seeing new ways of shaping learning institutions.

New technologies can free students from teacher domination and empower them to make their own meaning. Technologies can break through the brick classroom walls and open windows to the real world. Technologies, properly employed, may also liberate the teacher from pedantic roles, bringing out coaching and guiding talents that nurture the independence and imaginations of young learners.

Smokestack Research - Abysmal and Inconsequential

Under the smokestack paradigm, student research generally has been a pretty miserable experience for both student and teacher. Perhaps that is why "term papers" and research assignments seem to be an annual rather than weekly or monthly events.

The smokestack teacher emphasizes "go find out about" research, topical research that mainly requires students to find and move information. Little original thinking or imagination is required. Such research usually begins with a list of such topics as:

Dolly Madison

Mercantilism

The Battle of Bunker Hill

Crispus Attucks

The student goes to a library, pulls out an encyclopedia or book, and starts copying information and adult insights onto note cards, being careful to change a word in every sentence so as to avoid charges of plagiarism. The note cards filled, the student moves the words back onto lined paper or turns to a word processor to generate a personal "rendering" of the information. In most cases, because the research is not aimed toward answering some "essential," thought-provoking question, the student need not engage in analysis, synthesis, or evaluation to any significant degree.

This kind of research is little more than regurgitation. It has a close ally in the chapter review test, where students are expected to parrot back the insights shared by a teacher in countless lectures dutifully recorded in notebooks for memorization and recitation. In both of these experiences the student is not making meaning.

In some cases, the data and information available to students are archaic and inaccurate. Print materials often seem to hang around in school libraries for decades. Check the foreign country collections of your libraries, for example. What percentage are 10 years old? 15 years old? 20 years old? When students go to the library to do research on countries, what are they really learning?

INFORMATION AGE RESEARCH: POWERFUL PUZZLING ABOUT ESSENTIAL QUESTIONS

Students should do research on questions that matter to them, questions that require original thought and inspire a degree of passion. Questions that touch the core issues of what it means to be alive—what the Coalition of Essential Schools calls "essential questions" (Sizer, 1992)—drive student research with such power that parents sometimes must unplug computers, set curfews, and hold students back.

The Information Age teacher guides students through the questioning process to collect data and then analyze for patterns, turning data into information. The essential question hovers above the entire gathering and analyzing process, ultimately requiring the student to invent new meanings (synthesis) and propose novel solutions or choices (evaluation).

For example, after reading about Benedict Arnold, a student begins to wonder just what it takes to push someone past patriotism and loyalty to betray one's own land. Instead of merely describing the events of Arnold's betrayal, the student attempts an analysis and portrayal of Arnold's eroding personal commitment, identifying key incidents and events that might have "tipped the balance" toward betrayal. In a final section of the report, the student writes a policy paper, simulating advice to General Washington earlier in the war outlining and evaluating several options Washington can pursue to keep Arnold loyal.

Technology plays a critically important role in guiding this student's thinking. CD-ROM documents allow the student to do extensive word-searching to locate key sentences and paragraphs in hundreds of books, diaries, letters, and Colonial newspapers without having to physically scan them. Two or three hours of such scanning produces rich veins of information to support hypothesis testing. Prior to electronic information technologies, the same process might have required several weeks of searching through microfilms, with one hand taking notes and the other cranking the film.

The technology also supports a much more powerful kind of note-taking than was possible with cards. The student cuts and pastes key ideas and passages from the readings into a note-taking software program, which is more of an idea machine than a stack of cards. The software permits dynamic searching and sorting, the actual synthesis of puzzle pieces in new arrangements that ultimately flow into an outlining program, which supports the student in creating a report.

A middle-school student studying countries in Africa wants to figure out if any country is doing a better than expected job of reducing infant mortality and why it might be so. The investigation leads quickly to online databases or *PEMD*'s CD-ROM disc, which can provide data on infant mortality stretching back for decades and all the way up to this month. These data are downloaded and imported into *DataDesk*™, a statistics package with great visual power. The student is able to create a graph that quickly identifies an anomaly, one country that stands out from the pack.

To find out why that country stands out, the student conducts a search of world newspapers (in English), which turns up dozens of articles about infant mortality and Africa. The student downloads these articles, reads them and begins to generate a list of hypotheses to explain the anomaly. The student returns now to the databases to collect data, which can be imported into the statistical package to determine correlations between infant mortality rates and such factors as GNP per capita, number of doctors per 100,000 people, dollars spent per capita on medicine, etc.

Supplementing the search of print and numerical data, the student searches through the hundreds of thousands of visual images and video clips now available through videodiscs, listening to interviews, noting living conditions and converting the "left side of the brain" information into a more fully balanced perspective that allows the emotions and cultures of Africa to seep into consciousness.

Still not content, the student develops a pen pal relationship with more than a dozen African students, using the school modem to tie into some international bulletin boards. These students are eager to share their own perspectives on the essential question of keeping babies alive, and one student is able to convince both parents to send extensive letters that draw on their medical careers to provide insight into the challenge in their own community. When the student presents the final product or performance, he orchestrates a multimedia report that combines visuals of children, families, and hospitals with African music from a CD and a poetic narrative. This converts the facts, figures, and graphs, which have been printed by the computer and are in the hands of all classmates, into a dramatically personal story that leaves several young men and women in the class teary-eyed.

"I have decided to present this report to our congressperson," the student confides at the end. "I am very unhappy that our aid to Africa has been declining for the past decade, and I want to see a change."

CONCLUSION

New technologies can liberate this generation of students to become independent thinkers and problem-solvers, setting them loose in a new kind of educational playground—the playground of ideas and information. New technologies can immunize students against what Toffler (1991) calls the "info-tactics" of powerful groups and leaders who would manipulate the public toward their own selfish ends. Once the full potential of these technologies is realized, the roles of teachers can shift, the cultures of schools can open, and the basic assumptions that have blocked change for decades can be challenged. We can send a generation of "everyday heroes" out into the world, intent on improving it.

CHAPTER SEVEN

MEASURING RESULTS: WHAT HAPPENS TO STUDENT WRITING WITH THE WORD PROCESSOR?

A survey of research describing the impact of word processing on student writing often turns up confounding results. One Canadian study (Owston, 1990) concluded:

> *(1) the computer-written work was significantly better in overall quality and better on the competency and mechanics subscales of the evaluation instrument; (2) students produced significantly longer pieces of writing on the computer than off; (3) students reported very positive attitudes toward computer-based editing and writing; (4) there were no macrostructural differences in writing across media; and (5) only one surface feature, spelling, was found to be significantly better in the computer-written work. (ERIC abstract)*

In this particular study, the eighth-grade students had been using word processing for 1½ years. They preferred the computer and did somewhat better work when they used one. However, the study does not indicate how their writing—both on and off the word processor—might have changed for the better because of their 1½ years of using the technology.

51

There are several important issues that deserve attention from those who design writing programs using new technologies. There also are several issues of evaluation that deserve greater attention.

ISSUE #1: HAS THE SCHOOL, THE DEPARTMENT, OR THE DISTRICT IDENTIFIED IN EXPLICIT TERMS WHY AND HOW THE WORD PROCESSOR MIGHT RADICALLY ALTER THE QUALITY OF STUDENT WRITING?

All too often, the culture of past practice persists even with the new technology. In far too many computer labs, the word processor is employed like a glorified electronic typewriter. In such classrooms, the students often are blocked from composing early drafts and pre-writing on the word processor. They spend tedious moments transferring drafts onto the computer, frequently without the benefit of keyboarding skills. In addition, teachers who once restricted their written comments and corrections to issues of grammar and mechanics may well maintain that same practice with the word processor, emphasizing correctness rather than coherence, conviction, and clarity.

There was a time, not so long ago, when students in most writing classes first created an outline, then a draft in pencil, and finally a draft with pen or typewriter. Students rarely invested in revisions after receiving teacher comments, and it was often considered unwise to vary from the original outline. That outline controlled the flow of ideas much as steel rails keep a locomotive on track.

During the 1970s, *writing as process* pointed to a different view of writing, one which permitted a far longer period for incubation of ideas and thoughts. Writing as process emphasized multiple versions, flexibility, audience, non-linear thinking, and peer review. A basic tenet of this approach was the possibility that the best route to a good paper was not a straight line. In this approach, a writer was more like a gardener than a railroad engineer (Goldberg, 1984).

Combined with the word processor, writing as process offers the prospect of *idea processing*. The word processor provides greater fluidity and flexibility than other writing technologies. It supports greater word play and association. The writer can try out dozens, even hundreds of variations until the resulting product is just right. The word processor actually makes thinking more powerful, *as long as students are taught how to use it in that way.*

Unfortunately, the word processor works little magic by itself. If the mechanics-driven approach to writing still dominates a school and department, the word processor will do little more than improve the appearance and mechanics of student writing.

ISSUE #2: IS THE STAFF PREPARED TO EMPLOY THE WORD PROCESSOR AS AN IDEA PROCESSOR?

Unless teachers have had personal experience with the ways in which word processors may alter the processing of ideas, it is unlikely that they will know how to show those ways to their students. Through no fault of their own, they may have grown up with the "railroad school" of writing instruction and know little about circular thinking.

If a district expects word processing to work wonders, staff development in the writing as process approach is of paramount importance. Staff development should be conducted with word processors to demonstrate how ideas may be constructed, broken down, reconstructed, elaborated, extended, condensed, and amplified. As teachers of writing see their own thinking pass through stages of development in the fluidity of the screen, they will grasp the challenge of today's writing teacher—how best to lead students through similar stages of development.

As with so many other issues facing schools today, idea processing requires a paradigm shift. Strong writing thrives when minds are free to toy with many possibilities. This kind of word play is most likely to emerge when the writer or thinker works with fragments, rather than with completed sentences. Those taught in the railroad school of writing often feel compelled to spin out sentence after sentence in a logical flow, without having to retract words or circle back. This effort placed tremendous pressure on the thinker and often produced "writer's block," a condition of high anxiety preventing words from coming to mind.

In the writing as process approach, fragments are collected as beautiful beads, which later might be strung in some ordered sequences. There is no early pressure for order and logic. The emphasis is on richness. The goal is to gather as many impressions, thoughts, and insights as possible without feeling constrained by critical and analytical judgments.

One excellent resource to guide a school, a district, or a department toward the kinds of writing programs that take advantage of the word processor as an idea processor is the "Macintosh Writing Resource Guide" (1990) available from Apple Computer. This publication provides an extensive profile of schools that are conducting such programs, as well as a list of articles, books, consultants, and materials that emphasize writing as process.

ISSUE #3: DO STUDENTS HAVE SUFFICIENT ACCESS TO COMPUTERS SO THEY CAN DEVELOP THEIR IDEAS APPROPRIATELY OVER TIME?

Unfortunately, because access to computer labs can be somewhat limited, the ability to employ the word processor effectively as an idea processor may be related to home ownership of a computer. For ideas to gather, pass through an incubation period, and then receive the kind of careful attention they deserve, the student really needs many hours spread out over time. It is difficult to perform such writing during 30 to 40 minute segments once each day or several times each week.

Concern for equity suggests the importance of providing sustained access to computers at times other than during English class. Some schools have provided portables for students to take home. Others have kept their computer labs open outside the normal school schedule. Sometimes this has meant evening hours; other times it is a matter of adding afternoon hours. In any case, periodic surveys of students will uncover relationships between patterns of use and home ownership. If these surveys show that there is wide variation in who uses the computer for writing, the school has a responsibility to close the gap.

ISSUE #4: IS FORM MORE IMPORTANT THAN SUBSTANCE? IS LESS MORE?

Many studies point to the fluency with which students express themselves on the word processor (Apple Computer, 1990). After decades of complaining that students seemed almost constipated when it came to writing, one of the first victories of the word processor was the release of student words in torrents which filled page after electronic page.

Unfortunately, verbosity is not a desirable outcome. Expansive expression is fine as an early stage of idea processing, but we should be showing our students how to write concise prose that moves quickly and strongly to the point. We should show them how the word processor can support evaluation of their first thoughts so the young writers may increase clarity and impact. What we need is a major commitment to teaching students how to revise material.

"How long must it be?"

"Write an essay of at least 1,000 words . . ."

We must reconsider the messages we have expressed for much of this century. The job of writing is complete when the ideas have been expressed with clarity and impact. We should stop confusing quantity with quality. Too many students take our length requirements as a challenge to fill blank space, not recognizing that excess words provide a kind of blankness that is worse than white paper.

It would be better if we gave students other criteria for their writing. Request strong evidence to bolster arguments. Underline the importance of carefully chosen words. Stress the value of sentences that flow from one to another with a clarity that supports the essay's argument. Communicate your belief that less is often more. Challenge them to distill their thinking. No wine before its time!

"But I have read through, corrected all the spelling, and changed anything which sounded awkward!"

How often our students complain that there is little more than the above to change in their writing. This is most likely a sign that they need an expanded tool kit of editing strategies and questions. To be effective editors of their own work, they must be skilled at self-evaluation. They must be good questioners. They must analyze their first drafts to see where the sentence structure might be improved, where the logic might be strengthened, where the word choice might be more compelling, where the clarity might be sharpened, and where the perspective might be deepened. They must learn to employ peers as audience, reflecting on their reactions to early drafts before turning to a final version.

Analysis and *evaluation* point the way to *synthesis,* rearrangement of elements to create a better version. Students can learn to SCAMPER, that is, to employ a series of synthesis strategies developed by Robert Eberle (Michalko, 1991). Each letter of SCAMPER stands for a strategy. S = substitute. C = combine. A = adapt. M = modify, minify, magnify. P = put to other uses. E = eliminate. R = reverse. When students are hard-pressed to see how things might be altered, teach them to SCAMPER on the words and sentences of their early drafts.

To reach its full potential, editing must be reconceptualized across the curriculum to emphasize its role in "making meaning." Whether it be social studies, science, or math class, there is value in challenging students to make meaning out of the often confusing data that swirl around us during the Age of Information.

Just as writing provides a way to order one's thinking, to puzzle things out, to make connections between seemingly unrelated fragments, editing is an essential stage in the development of ideas and in the communication of those ideas. When converting *data* into *information* and then into *insight,* editing becomes especially important. Editing permits focus and provides perspective. The puzzle otherwise remains blurred. Nonsense and chaos prevail.

To equip all students with the ability to convert raw data into insight, departments should collaborate to give students experiences with raw data. Writing as a vehicle for thinking should become a schoolwide focus and commitment in order to address the national deficit in reasoning abilities, documented by the series of Report Cards flowing out of the NAEP (National Assessment of Educational Progress) in recent years. The NAEP has shown that fewer than 10% of 11th-graders taking the tests can demonstrate high levels of reasoning, whether it be in writing persuasive essays or performing scientific reasoning (Jones, et. al., 1992; and Applebee, et. al., 1986).

A schoolwide commitment to writing for thinking and writing as process would require agreement among teachers on the stages of development of an idea as a student moves from raw data to insight. Teachers need to become guides who show young people how to make the journey from uncertainty and curiosity through theory-testing to the development and expression of tentative conclusions. Teachers need to help students to see the interplay between thinking and word play. Sentence structure and logic become partners, rather than opponents. Poetry belongs in the math and science paper as much as the English paper, as metaphor and the flow of language help to express the elegance of scientific and mathematical theories and principles.

ISSUE # 5: HOW DO WE KNOW THAT WRITING IS IMPROVING?

We need evaluation designs that match our goals; but we also must acknowledge that the most important intervention of all is the writing method itself, not the technology.

Teaching writing with the railway approach will make little use of the word processor's special potential. Conversely, writing as process will exploit the technology to its fullest. At the same time, once a writer learns word play with the computer, she or he is likely to transform the old technologies of pencil and paper, for example, outlining ideas for writing with word webs when wielding a pencil.

As the Canadian study (Owston, 1990), quoted in the beginning of this article, found, "there were no macrostructural differences in writing across media." Good thinking and writing, once learned, surface with pencil and paper as well as with the computer. The wise teacher shows students how to perform word play on the screen of the *mind's eye* so as to guard against undue reliance on the new electronic version. Otherwise, students might be unduly handicapped in a society that persists in testing students with blue composition booklets rather than computers.

Once we have identified the characteristics of effective writing, we should construct district evaluation procedures to trace the development of those characteristics over time. We also should use that data to evaluate the programs we use. Student portfolios maintained throughout the K-12 experience provide good research data to explore important questions about program impact. We can look at specific programs and how they have influenced the development of student writing.

Take, for example, the goal of improving student editing skills with regard to *word choice*. If one group of students has received intensive practice on this skill throughout the year and a second group is serving as a control group, how can we measure the effectiveness of the program? We can collect early writings and count how many words have been "upgraded" between early drafts and the final drafts. When counting "upgrades," evaluators must agree on criteria that reward only changes that fit the context. The number of upgrades then can be divided by the total number of words in the final draft to establish a basis for comparison that reflects quality as well as quantity. We then can explore the following questions:

1) Have students in the word-choice program increased the frequency of appropriate word replacement to a statistically significant extent?

2) Is the change in the frequency of appropriate word replacement greater or smaller in the control group vs. those in the word-choice program?

In a similar fashion, we can seek evidence of improved *coherence* by identifying changes in the sequencing of ideas from early drafts to later drafts. We can look for evidence of improved transitions, the introduction of parallelism, and the modification of sentence structure. If we care about macro-structural changes, we must devote attention to evaluation procedures that track these developments.

CONCLUSION

Even though the word processor promises much, delivering on those promises requires significant program changes that extend far beyond the installation of computers in a lab facility.

In order to see whether the promises are fulfilled, districts need to establish evaluation programs that are matched to the established goals. The purpose of such evaluations, at least in part, should be to provide data to steer the programs forward with insight rather than blind faith. Careful program assessment, combining qualitative measures as well as quantitative data, can inspire program changes that will lead to better results. Assessment also can broaden the base of community and board support for expanded commitments to technology as a tool to support improved student reasoning and performance.

CHAPTER EIGHT

THE SAGA OF AMY AND SUSAN: A "FUTURE PERFECT" ILS

An integrated learning system (ILS) holds great promise in a "future perfect" sense. Unfortunately, the trouble with educational technologies, as with much planning for the future, is the tendency of most organizations to move into the future with visions limited by old paradigms and patterns of behavior (Davis, 1987). Instead of introducing ILS systems that truly revolutionize the learning of students, we see systems that emulate smokestack learning. Instead of ILS systems that empower students to perform higher-level thinking, we see systems tightly correlated to standardized tests, which set low expectations for student reasoning. ILS systems can deliver highly customized, diagnostic, and prescriptive instruction. However, most systems in schools move students along relatively crude learning paths in primarily linear fashion; they are not adapted to individual learning styles, and have extremely limited corrective interventions.

If we reach into the future to the year 2000 and ask what an integrated learning system might do for student learning, we end up with a very different system than what we now see on the market. Unfortunately, it seems that many vendors have failed to read either Davis' book or the story of Jack and

61

the beanstalk. Both Davis and Jack understood the importance of magic beans to those who wish to reach the sky.

Let's begin by challenging some of the old paradigms, which so often seem to hold us back from realizing technology's potential.

The first paradigm is the notion that *practice is the equivalent of learning.* Related to the practice paradigm is the *more is better paradigm:* "The more you practice the better you get."

A remarkably large number of existing remedial programs are built on this notion. One begins by dividing reading or math into thousands of discrete skills. You then find out which of those skills the student has not mastered. You purchase thousands of pages of ditto sheets closely tied to those discrete skills, and you condemn the remedial student to a dozen years of practice.

What is the cure rate for remedial students? What percentage leaves the remedial program for successful integration into the regular classroom?

The basic flaw in this kind of program is the assumption that "practice makes perfect." Practice is not the same as learning. This paradigm assumes that it is the educator's job to teach students rules and patterns (scripts) rather than real problem-solving and reasoning. Rote learning and learning rules might have suited an industrial society, but they make little sense in an Age of Information, which will require a very large percentage of our citizens to be brainworkers.

True remediation equips students with new thinking tools that allow dramatic shifts in performance. The student learns to think about her or his own thinking patterns. He or she learns to create new scripts when the old ones cease to work well.

Good teachers always have sought to empower students to "make their own meaning," another way of referring to writing their own scripts. When a student displays a pattern of errors, the good teacher tries to bring the student thinking out into the open, where it may be examined. Unfortunately, teachers operating under the practice paradigm rarely take the time to encourage such reflection. Wrong patterns often persist. The learning system remains virtually undisturbed.

An integrated learning system ought to solve this problem by teaching students to be script writers and problem solvers, rather than script followers with little skill to tackle anything above a two-step word problem.

But what actually happens when students log onto one of the current ILS programs? Make a wrong response and most programs ask you to "try again." If you persist in making a wrong answer, many programs supply the right answer and move you on to the next item. Some programs will provide a prompt or clue to guide your thinking; but if you still persist in making a wrong answer, most of these programs give up and send you forward.

Once in a while, you may find a program that recognizes the fact that you just do not seem to understand. This program halts the forward progression and teaches you a lesson (script) to match the item with which you are having problems. This lesson is a basic explanation of how your mind is supposed to be working. Once complete, you are back to more practice.

What happens if you still have problems with the practice items? The best I have seen thus far is a second and third exposure to the same explanatory lesson.

A great teacher watches for such patterns of errors and helps the student break the pattern and make meaning. This teacher has a repertoire of instructional strategies that touches all learning styles. This teacher does not simply repeat the same explanation over and over, louder and louder. The goal is to help the student understand the process, not just memorize it. That is what computers and ILS should do.

The philosophical and psychological paradigm underlying this kind of learning is "constructivism." The learner constructs meaning as she or he passes through life. The learner writes the scripts and re-writes the scripts until they work. The teacher helps the learner acquire the script editing and writing skills. Ultimately, the learner becomes quite independent, what often is called "a lifelong learner."

How might a "future perfect" integrated learning system support the development of such thinkers and learners? It would begin by establishing clear goals:

1) It is the job of such software to produce thinkers and script writers, rather than automatons.

2) It is the job of such software to equip students with tool kits that support inventive thinking.

3) It is the job of such software to encourage reflection about thinking and problem solving.

4) It is the job of the computer to customize the learning experience to match the needs of the learner, providing a rich menu of learning options likely to optimize the speed and depth with which the learner acquires new skills and capacities.

These goals suggest software that would act in the following ways:

Time on the computer would be devoted largely to problem-solving and real-life applications, rather than isolated practice. These problems would flow out of a "whole learning" approach. Instead of segmenting skills into thousands of separate pieces, each with their own practice experiences, the student would be asked to apply arrays of skills to more complex problems requiring a balanced and holistic approach. These problems would not step up to be solved in perfectly ordered patterns, matching some publisher's conception of appropriate skill development. They would appear with some of the surprise and randomness characteristic of real life. The student's own curiosity also might be a driving force in the selection process.

Many of these problems—as is true of problems in real life—would be somewhat new to the student, though all would have some familiar elements. The software would provide guidance and support to the student as she or he moves toward solution. "Help" would always be an available option. If the student does not have the foggiest notion of where to begin, she or he might ask for a hint.

"Where do I start with this one?" asks Amy. The computer (which has been named "Susan" by Amy) has been watching this particular student solve problems for more than two years. Like any good tutor, the computer remembers recent struggles with understanding problem-solving procedures. Using basic artificial intelligence systems and voice recognition, the computer has learned a great deal about the development of Amy's learning capacities.

"Do you remember Polya's basic problem-solving strategies? (Polya, 1964) Perhaps one of those would help you get started?"

Amy frowns and searches her memory. "Don't tell me!" she whispers fiercely. "Let's see if I can remember."

Susan, the computer, remains silent.

Amy easily remembers "chunking," her favorite. "I like that one because it makes big problems into little problems."

She asks herself which "heuristic" would be helpful for this particular problem and ends up shaking her head.

"Draw a picture?" She tries some sketches on Susan's tablet but finds little insight emerging. "Well, maybe one of the others I've forgotten will help me more. Could you show me the list again to refresh my memory?"

Susan meets the request with the first two Amy has remembered at the top of the list.

"Analogous reasoning?" quizzes Amy. "What does that mean? I don't remember that one."

The computer's screen changes to a definition and an example. "Look for elements in this problem that are something like problems you have encountered in the past and see if there is a strategy that helped you then which might be helpful with this problem."

"Oh yeah, I remember now. That just might work." Amy proceeds to apply different problem-solving strategies until the knot loosens and a solution comes into view.

"And what did you learn about problem-solving today?" Susan asks.

"Oh really, Susan, do we have to go through that again?"

Susan again remains silent.

"You're remaining silent. Smart! Who says computers are stupid? I know all the arguments about my making up my own mind and learning about learning. It's just that sometimes I wish I could let you give me all the insights and answers, like teachers used to in those old-fashioned schools."

"As a special treat, Amy, I will replay history for you this one time." The computer takes on a serious, professorial tone: "Now, class, today we have seen the power of Polya's fourth problem-solving strategy, analogous reasoning . . . "

"No! Stop! Enough! I'd rather do it myself."

66

Amy completes the metacognitive exercise and then selects a learning adventure from a recently upgraded menu.

"I'd like to practice my negotiating skills. Let's go back in history to the time when Columbus was about to launch his second trip to the New World. I want to play the role of Isabella." Amy frowns. "No, on second thought, let's try the sale of Manhattan. I want to play the role of the Native Americans and see if I can win a better deal."

The computer asks Amy what information she would like before playing the simulation.

"Let's start with background concerning each of the key players. I especially want to know something about the interests, personalities, and culture of the Colonists. How do they play this negotiating game? Do they ever play dirty? What are the communication patterns that may prove confusing?"

Susan hesitates for a few nanoseconds while searching several hundred databases, and then the screen fills with the grimly serious face of the leading negotiator. He is standing with an armful of blankets and jackets. The computer begins sharing a profile of this historical figure in a professorial voice.

"Sorry, Susan, but I'd rather read the text of your comments. I can read faster silently and stop to think while I am reading. If I *was* going to listen to you, I would insist upon a different voice. Really! That stuffy voice is a bore."

Once Amy has done her homework and studied her opponents, she asks to see a replay of the actual negotiations—30 minutes of highlights. This done, she initiates a strategy session.

"I want to develop a strategy, Susan. Can you give me a list of prompts to help me think about this upcoming session? Let's try the *Getting to Yes* model."

Some of you will recognize parts of the *Knowledge Navigator* video circulated by Apple a few years back. The paradigm is simple: *All students can learn. All children can learn to reason.* and *An integrated learning system can provide the data, information, and thinking tutorials to support the development of students' script-writing and independent problem-solving.*

How practical is this "future perfect" concept of ILS? We already have most of the pieces required to produce these kinds of learning experiences. Cathleen Wilson of Bank Street developed a prototype for RCA several years ago. Called "Palenque," it allows a student to explore the Mayan ruin "at will," as if standing on the grounds themselves (Wilson, 1992).

What we lack is the commitment, the market, and the funding. As long as the smokestack paradigms dominate education, publishers will keep turning out smokestack products. They are afraid that there will be no market for radical new products.

ILS is an idea whose time has come, but the prototypes currently available fall far short of their promise. If we truly wish to become "Number One" in math and science by the year 2000, we will need script-writers, not script-followers. Let's see the nation put some dollars behind development of an ILS system that is "future perfect," one which will help produce a generation of "brain workers" and independent problem-solvers.

CHAPTER NINE

THE GREAT DEBATE: ARE CAI AND ILS WORTH THE INVESTMENT?

A careful review of the research might cause many people to hesitate before investing large sums in integrated learning systems or computer-assisted instruction (CAI). While there are dozens of studies claiming miracle results for ILS, it is difficult to find *well-designed studies* that report such significant improvements in student performance.

Henry J. Becker's review of the research (1988) is worth quoting at some length:

> In order to prepare a best-evidence synthesis on the effects of computer-based instructional programs on children's learning, we began a search for empirical research about the effects of computer-based approaches on basic curricular categories of learning (math, language arts, writing, science, etc.) in grades 1 through 12. We limited the search to reports produced since 1984 and including achievement measures as outcomes.

> The 51 reports that were obtained included 11 dissertations, 13 reports of school district evaluations, 15 published articles, and 12 unpublished papers.

69

Of the 51 studies, 11 were eliminated because they had no comparison group, and measures of effects were limited to gains on standardized achievement tests over varying periods of time.

Of the remaining 40 studies, eight were excluded from consideration because they did not employ pre-test controls and neither classes nor students were randomly assigned. Lacking both pre-tests and random assignment, it was impossible to equate the computer-using groups and the traditional instruction groups.

Seven more studies were removed because the treatment period was shorter than eight weeks and, finally, we chose not to consider eight studies involving fewer than 40 children, or where each treatment involved only a single class of students and the experimental and control classes were taught by different teachers.

What about the major element of experimental design—random assignment? Of the remaining studies, only one randomly assigned pupils to classes, which were in turn randomly assigned to computer-assigned or traditional treatments.

It is not unusual to attend a session at a national meeting during which a proponent of ILS distributes copies of graphs showing dramatic student results, though the study would not pass any of Becker's tests. It also is not unusual for vendors to distribute such graphs as "evidence" to justify huge expenditures.

If experimental design means anything, it is a set of standards designed to ascertain whether the study effects actually result from the intervention itself, rather than from such circumstances as the high quality of volunteer instructors, the students, or the well-documented "Hawthorne effect"

(Campbell and Stanley, 1963). Why do so many educators and vendors suspend these standards? At times this scenario seems reminiscent of "The Emperor's New Clothes."

Another meta-analysis of student learning with computer-based instruction (Kulik and Kulik, 1989) claims that students "generally learned more in classes in which they received computer-based instruction. The average effect of computer-based instruction in all 254 studies with examination results was to raise examination scores by 0.30 standard deviations, or from the fiftieth to the sixty-second percentile."

Even though the Kuliks report positive effects, they note several discrepant findings that deserve attention:

1) Study results were more positive for published studies than they were for unpublished studies.

2) Study results were more positive when control and experimental groups were taught by different teachers than when taught by the same teachers.

3) Study results were more positive for short studies than they were for long studies.

4) There were no significant differences between true experimental studies and quasi-experimental studies.

They pose four main hypotheses for these findings: editorial gate-keeping, experimental design flaws, novelty effect, and instructional quality.

What seems missing from this kind of meta-analysis is research comparing the relative effects of various investments. For example, given a choice of spending a million dollars on ILS systems as opposed to staff training in instructional strategies, which pays the greatest dividends? Which is better for students, access to computer training or access to a human tutor?

In a 1991 update of their research, Kulik and Kulik acknowledge this hole in the research:

> *Finally, this meta-analysis produced no evidence on what is certainly one of the most important questions of all about computer-based instruction (CBI): Is it cost effective? An early analysis by Levin, Destner, & Meister (1986) had suggested that the costs of CBI were too great given its record of effectiveness. Levin et. al. suggested that nontechnological innovations, such as tutoring, produced results that were just as good at a lower cost. Later reanalyses, such as those by Blackwell, Niemiec and Walberg (1986), have suggested that computer-based instruction is not only a cost effective alternative to traditional instruction but that it is far more cost effective than such non-technological innovations as tutoring.*

Unfortunately, there is hardly any research available to answer these kinds of questions. Most districts seem to go one way or another. Few seem willing to set up a true experiment with some students working with computers, others working with well trained teachers, and still others remaining in traditional programs.

Becker (1988) and others have called for a fresh approach to research in this area, and one might expect the federal government to take a more active role in organizing such balanced studies. It may be too much to expect objectivity from vendors.

Any district considering adoption of CAI or ILS might try the following strategies to help evaluate the claims made by vendors:

1. Ask for a complete list of districts that have tried the program. When vendors display their victories, they should also reveal their embarrassments. Careful telephone inquiries can help cut through the hype and sales

pitches to find out what people really think, although it is often difficult to find administrators willing to admit million-dollar mistakes.

2. Ask for written evaluation reports directly from those districts showing student outcomes, staff attitudes, etc.; look for statistically significant changes; and read the fine print. Sometimes statistically significant changes may amount to a handful of extra correct responses. Translate the numbers into tangible results.

3. Assess the bias of the principal evaluating team. Do they have a stake in the outcome, or are they independent and uninvolved?

4. Check to see if evaluation designs included comparable control groups and meaningful pre- and post-testing.

5. Ask for results over time (3 to 4 years). There is some evidence that early effects fade over time as the novelty wears off. Many reports available from vendors report only a single year.

6. Translate the total annual cost of the program (including staff development, maintenance, etc.) into an equivalent number of staff positions or hours of participation in staff-development programs to appreciate true (opportunity) cost.

Given the fact that few districts have all of the equipment they would like to own, the ultimate issue is whether or not CAI and ILS are the best uses of information technologies. If students have limited access, how might they best spend their time? Is reading practice more valuable than learning to compose on the word processor? When does a student learn the information skills Toffler says are essential to citizenship in the Information Age? Until ILS can deliver reasoning and problem-solving at a higher level, I would vote for such applications as database searches and statistical analysis, which put powerful tools for problem-solving in student hands.

CHAPTER TEN

DESIGNING STAFF DEVELOPMENT FOR NEW TECHNOLOGIES

"What business do English teachers have teaching word processing? That belongs in the business department!"

Teachers trained in one technology and mind-set sometimes find themselves gridlocked into old patterns and perceptions. Thrust into a world of new technologies, they persist in seeing them in terms of the familiar; the word processor, for example, is viewed as a glorified typewriter with powerful editing features, rather than as the idea processor it can be. To understand the computer's power for idea processing and improved composition, one must take a computer home, live with it, and write with it. Only by embracing the technology can one experience the kind of immersion that breaks through the surface understandings to a deeper level of involvement:

"I used to have a problem with 'writer's block.' The word processor changed all that. And my students report that their ideas flow more smoothly at first writing. They worry about word choice and coherence at a later stage. Word processing is different from writing with a pencil."

Whether it be learning to teach for thinking, to deliver lessons within a cooperative learning framework, or to master such new technologies as videodiscs and multimedia, the traditional conceptions of staff development must be reconsidered and revised to support the kinds of adult learning that will bring educators enthusiastically to the cutting edge of practice without encountering the bleeding edge.

TRADITIONAL STAFF DEVELOPMENT—A DISMAL TRACK RECORD

How do teachers learn to become pioneers, inventors, and shapers of the new culture, rather than the transmitters of the old? How do they come to employ the new technologies with the same degree of comfort and skill as they currently employ chalk and chalkboard?

First, we must acknowledge that the required metamorphosis is as profound as the change from caterpillar to butterfly. Shifting from Industrial Age thinking and teaching to Information Age thinking and teaching is a dramatic adjustment, especially if the role of the teacher shifts from "sage on the stage" to "guide on the side."

The training agenda is no simple list of skills; everybody must learn entirely new approaches to the making and sharing of meaning within classrooms. The teacher becomes a guide and coach showing students how to navigate through the complex information resources now available at the click of a mouse.

To support such fundamental change, schools need to apply a different model of adult learning from the one that has governed staff development for decades. The historical solution to the problem of changing teacher behaviors—traditional staff development—cannot begin to meet this challenge. At its worst, traditional staff development was a waste of time and resources. Unfortunately, the prevailing norms for technology-related training cause districts to rely too frequently on just such traditional practices.

EFFECTIVE STAFF DEVELOPMENT

Staff development can make a powerful difference in the performance of both students and teachers. According to Joyce and Showers (1983), effective programs require carefully structured, ongoing efforts based on the research on effective practices and sustained with proper funding. Participants must be equipped to cope with what Joyce calls the "challenge of transfer," which refers to the difficulty of actually translating any new set of skills and practices into routine and comfortable classroom use.

Traditional staff development relied too much on theory, practice, and demonstration that were distinct from the classroom setting. Effective practices devote considerable attention to the crossing of this bridge, warning participants of the challenge in advance and then supporting them through the process. It uses, among other things, peer coaching and support groups to encourage perseverance and eventual success. None of this is possible with the traditional, one-shot, short-term, skill-based training programs. Without such support systems, the new skills and behaviors have difficulty taking root in the classroom.

As teachers learn new skills and attitudes, they should consider the obstacles to making these skills work in their classrooms. Before trying the new skills in their classrooms, teachers should have ample opportunity to practice the skills in relatively controlled and safe environments until a significant degree of confidence and skill has been acquired. Over succeeding weeks and months, "coaching" by peers and sustained practice are essential if the new approaches are to take root. The goal is the eventual development of "executive control"—a level of skillful use that is smooth, effective, comfortable, and routine (Joyce and Showers, 1983).

STAFF DEVELOPMENT FOR NEW TECHNOLOGIES

To develop a technologically competent and literate teaching force during the coming decade, the following principles deserve careful attention:

1. *The district technology, curriculum, and staff-development committees should collaborate to clarify expectations for technological literacy and to establish a five-year offering of technology-related courses.*

   Technological literacy means much more than the ability to employ a particular set of software packages. Teachers of the Information Age must have a broader understanding of how information and technologies will be used to support the making of meaning and the solving of problems. District committees should concur on an explicit list of the teacher understandings and proficiencies that constitute literacy and then plan staff-development programs that will guarantee such literacy across the entire staff within a reasonable period of time.

2. *The learning of new technologies should attend to the challenge of transferring use to the teacher's classroom.*

   While many districts have provided a full menu of courses to acquaint teachers with various software programs, there is considerable evidence that teachers have not seen how to make use of those programs to include appropriate experiences in their classrooms (Cuban, 1992). They may learn how to do a spreadsheet, for example, without anyone showing them how it could be used to empower student thinking with regard to data. All too often, the instructor is skilled in the use of the software but ignorant of its potential to shift the way students and teachers might work together in various disciplines. The district must invest in researching appropriate applications of technologies to each of the disciplines and make certain that such findings are integrated into the staff-development program. Social studies, science, and other teachers deserve a chance to see models of technology integration.

3. *The learning of new technologies should strengthen the instructional strategies identified as appropriate by the district's long-range educational plan.*

Although many districts pass forward-thinking educational plans that call for a change in classrooms to empower the learner and emphasize real-life applications, they rarely construct adult learning experiences consistent with those visions. Technology learning experiences should mirror the kinds of instructional strategies advocated by such visions. For example, if problem-solving is a district theme, the technology course might begin with participants being formed into teams confronted by a challenge that can only, it turns out, be solved by using new technologies. Subsequent skill learning will then follow in response to an appetite and a purpose.

4. *The learning of new technologies should offer many different options for differing learning styles and levels of development.*

There are significant differences in the ways adults prefer to learn anything, and the most effective programs offer choices to allow learners to match style with experience. As long as the proficiencies attached to technological literacy are clearly expressed and measured, it matters little which path individuals select. All too often, districts offer nothing but formal training sessions, though we know that many people learn new technologies collaboratively or individually. Too often, 20 or more teachers sit in a computer lab and are led through a prescribed sequence of steps, which holds some back and frustrates others. This practice reflects the preoccupation with the learning of software rather than the exploration of educational potential.

If our goal is to support the comfortable, skillful integration of technologies into regular classrooms, we must acknowledge that most teachers pass through stages from *survival* to *mastery* to *impact,* or substantial infusion into classroom activities (Mandinach, 1992). Mandinach calls the most-advanced stage *innovation,* in which a teacher goes well beyond "the mandated scope of the curriculum toward a complete restructuring of teaching and learning activities" (p. 12). The learning experiences offered to teachers must be varied enough to meet the different needs of people at various stages.

5. *The learning of new technologies should involve participants in the invention of classroom applications.*

Too many staff-development programs are built upon the assumption that teachers are only tool-users. Such programs present a package of skills and strategies to be learned and practiced by the teacher. Often these packages are promoted as being "teacher proof"; in other words, individual teachers cannot "mess things up." The implication is that the strategies will work in just about any classroom. Yet the wise teacher twists and changes the strategies (breaks and shapes the tools) to fit the special demands of Room 236. The novice returns to the classroom with a limited supply of effective classroom practices learned during the workshop, not knowing how to modify them to fit local conditions and not knowing how to construct new activities once that small supply is exhausted.

If we expect to see most teachers reach the mastery and innovation stages described by Mandinach, then invention must be made an explicit part of the technology staff-development experience.

6. *The learning of new technologies should involve participants in team-learning, both during and subsequent to actual workshops.*

Joyce (1988) has presented compelling evidence that the transfer of new techniques to the classroom is far more likely to occur when the teachers work in pairs and employ peer coaching. Technology programs should take advantage of such strategies to increase the likelihood that participants will achieve executive control. Also, cooperative learning reduces the isolation often associated with these technologies; and it models the kinds of technology uses we hope to see teachers employing with their students.

7. *The learning of new technologies should involve participants in experience-based opportunities, with learning resulting from doing and exploring.*

Teachers—like their students—too often sit passively listening to staff development messages. The assumption seems to be that one quick look at a new method or approach is sufficient to empower the audience to turn their classrooms upside down.

Substantial shifts in perspective and behavior depend on active involvement, experience, and role-playing. Although workshops using such methods will necessarily take longer than traditional workshops, this time investment will pay greater dividends for a longer time. Active involvement in exploration, which results from wrestling with experiences and attempting to integrate them into one's understanding, leads teachers to feel

81

more committed to the discoveries made and more comfortable with the process of changing perspective.

8. *The learning of new technologies should involve participants in questioning outmoded classroom paradigms.*

Because many of the new technologies make possible a more student-centered classroom, teachers must spend some time asking how their classroom practices might support such a shift. All too often, the new goals will be subverted by relatively subtle factors, such as the arrangement of classroom furniture that makes group work difficult and frustrating. If teachers can anticipate which classroom structures and traditions need shifting in advance of the actual experience, the chances of success are enhanced.

9. *Staff development must consider the feelings, fears, and anxieties of the learners.*

Many teachers will feel some degree of anxiety, especially when they are trying new technologies. Like novice scuba divers descending for the first time, teachers may experience heavier breathing and a sense of risk. Courses should be constructed with this phenomenon in mind. The instructor or group leader should have specific strategies for identifying anxious learners, as well as strategies for easing their anxieties.

For example, one staff developer found that one way to combat computer anxiety was to encourage name-calling. "Call the machine names!" she urged. The body language of the learners relaxed dramatically as they came to view the machine as a person or animal instead of some all-powerful technological marvel. When the learners were supported in their natural inclination to make the computer less threatening and less mystical, they made greater progress with the skills being taught.

Staff developers have noticed that many participants reach an early saturation point when covering new ground. Pacing becomes an essential issue. It pays to curtail grandiose expectations in favor of learner comfort. In teaching word processing, for example, it is wise to teach novices four or five commands in the first lesson, just enough to support them in creating an impressive document. Once they understand the commands, they should write and write until they announce, "This is easy!" Additional commands and skills are best introduced in small doses until the foundation of confidence has been firmly laid.

CONCLUSION

Now that we have collected compelling research about what kinds of staff development programs produce the greatest amount of transfer and student achievement, we no longer can persist with the old, ineffective models. Staff development for technologies can build on these successful models while reaching out to achieve a much greater level of connection with district vision statements. We must bear in mind that we are not teaching technology for its own sake. The goal is the effective employment of technologies in order to solve problems and make meaning.

CHAPTER ELEVEN

DESIGNING ENVIRONMENTS SUITED TO THE NEW TECHNOLOGIES

When new technologies make their first appearance, we often try to bend and adjust them to fit within pre-existing contexts and spaces,'thereby losing much of their potential. The functions of our programs follow the forms and dictates of the space, instead of the reverse. Form should follow from the functions.

Even when we have the opportunity to build a school from scratch or conduct a major renovation, old paradigms often act to block imaginative thinking about the best possible design.

Sometimes these new facilities—whether they are science labs, "shops," writing centers, or computer labs—show a remarkable resemblance to those of the 1950s. Smokestack thinking translates rapidly into smokestack design. The gleaming stainless steel diner of the 1950s has given way to new forms more rapidly than have school classrooms.

While not all of the following paradigms are held in all school districts, they can be found alive and well in a surprisingly large number of places. They nearly guarantee that when we visit a school, we can count on feeling right at home, on seeing rooms and spaces very much like the ones in the schools we attended decades ago.

The list below is not meant to be exhaustive, and the reader can probably add a good dozen or more from personal experience. The important question is how much longer will we permit this kind of thinking to block us from realizing our dreams?

SMOKESTACK PARADIGMS

1) Learning is best served by facing students toward a teacher.

2) Learning is best served by isolating students from one another.

3) Learning is best served by bolting things down.

4) Learning is best served by the least expensive versions of whatever is being placed within the space.

5) Learning is best served by rectangular spaces.

6) Learning is best served by employing architects who have virtually no knowledge of how the new technologies might be used.

7) Learning is best served by sticking with traditional design and asking few questions about possible variations.

8) Learning is best served by denying both teachers and students a say in the design.

9) Learning is best served by ignoring innovative exemplars during the design stage.

10) Learning is best served by ignoring analogous design challenges from such other spheres as industry .

11) Learning is best served by hiring the cheapest contractors.

12) Learning is best served by waiting to select a contractor until after the design is complete, thereby depriving the contractor of a say in the design.

13) Learning is best served by providing for only one use at a time in any space.

14) Learning is best served by building no excess capacity into spaces to provide for future expansion, modification, or innovation.

15) Learning is best served by selecting only those technologies that already have proven effective or only those technologies that are totally untested.

16) Learning is best served by instructional experiences and strategies that have been proven ineffective for decades.

17) Learning is best served in spaces isolated from other spaces.

18) Learning is best served by spaces that can be accessed easily only during the normal school day.

19) Learning is best served by spaces with inadequate security and cooling systems that restrict their use to certain times and months.

20) Learning is best served by technology packages created by outside experts.

Some readers may claim that this list is overly harsh, that it exaggerates the case. That may be so for those working with enlightened, forward-thinking groups; but it is a rare district that cannot identify a few of the paradigms as alive and well.

CREATING A DESIGN PARADIGM SHIFT

So what is one to do about this reality?

We begin by challenging the old paradigms, which seem to conflict with our educational philosophies, in order to replace them with new paradigms to guide our design process. If you serve on a district design team that is contemplating the development of new spaces for new technologies, take the above list of smokestack paradigms and ask members of your group to take a stand. With which do they agree? Which need replacement? Follow this activity by creating a list of those that most group members agree need changing. Hold a series of discussions to develop new ideas and values that may serve the district better during the next decade.

A group of inventive thinkers can move beyond smokestack design. For example, at one high school the design team included arts teachers of various kinds. Industrial arts, video production, student publications, and visual arts instructors put their minds together to create a workspace that violated many of the paradigms listed above. Their original design bias leaned heavily toward project work, student-centered learning, group production, and the flexible use of space.

SOME INFORMATION AGE PARADIGMS

1) Learning is best served when students can face in many different directions, according to the tasks they are performing. Sometimes this will mean facing a teacher or presenter (including other students) in various locations around the room. At other times it may mean facing a team of other students working to produce a product.

2) Learning is best served by using the number of individuals that makes sense for the task. At times this will mean working solo. At other times it may mean cooperative grouping.

3) Learning is best served by having multiple power and network access ports spaced frequently across the floor space, along with highly movable, modular furniture that can be shifted around to fit the functions that need to be performed. Very little should be bolted down. The technology center can be redesigned daily and weekly as the functions grow and the technologies mature.

4) Learning is best served by the technology that creates the maximum "bang for the buck." Over the long run, a faster, more powerful machine with color may be more cost effective because it reduces "wait time" by 90% or more and also supports a higher level of thinking and interpretation. If the test of good investment is the ROI (Return on Investment), we must ask which technologies and platforms will bring our students the greatest success as citizens and workers. Would we teach auto mechanics with Model T Fords?

5) Learning is best served by adapting the dimensions of spaces to fit the activities that will occur within them. Squares and circles are often better suited for collaboration than rectangles. Partitions can provide flexible dimensions.

6) Learning is best served by hiring architects who specialize in designing innovative spaces for new technologies in schools or other environments.

7) Learning is best served by challenging smokestack spacial designs and having greater respect for function and philosophy.

8) Learning is best served by involving teachers and students in the "future perfect" environmental design process, provided, of course, that such involvement does not merely replicate outdated perspectives and paradigms.

9) Learning is best served by getting out into the world to see what others are doing to marry space with new technologies.

10) Learning is best served by checking out analogous designs from industry and non-profit organizations.

11) Learning is best served by finding contractors who can be relied upon to create a space that meets the required standards, even though most state bidding laws may make this choice difficult. Careful attention to bid specifications and criteria (in advance) may help to exclude those who cannot demonstrate the required competencies and experience. Legal advice is definitely needed.

12) Learning is best served by engaging a trusted and experienced contractor as a paid advisor during the design stage. Architects often seem to lack the practical nuts-and-bolts knowledge possessed by a good contractor. The contractor can help keep costs down by explaining the impact of various choices.

13) Learning is best served by enabling dozens of different activities to occur within the same large space at the same time. Openness, generous capacity, and flexibility will minimize scheduling conflicts and maximize utilization.

14) Learning is best served by providing room for expansion and change. Opportunities to start renovation projects are too rare to limit design to this year's needs.

15) Learning is best served by conducting modest pilot programs for new technologies, thus maximizing opportunities to discover fresh approaches while minimizing risks.

16) Learning is best served by critically examining past practices in order to discard the ineffective and replace

them with learning experiences better suited to the preparation of citizens for the next century.

17) Learning is best served in spaces that flow naturally into other spaces, so that functions may flow across boundary lines in search of appropriate connections. Just as isolationism has given way to a global village on the international stage, ideas must be allowed to form and move within communities of learning without having to surmount unnatural boundaries of discipline and turf. If the task of the Information Age is to help students make connections on their way to making meaning, spaces should support that search for meaning.

18) Learning is best served by spaces that are open and accessible, either physically or electronically, for 24 hours a day. The information and technology resources of the school should be viewed as community property. Groups should be free to move through the facility during much of the day and evening, coaching each other and swapping stories, wisdom, or questions. Artificial age barriers should be dismantled so that youth learn from elders and elders learn from youth.

19) Learning is best served by creating a comfortable climate for technology throughout the entire year. Even though the initial investment may seem prohibitive, a 20% increase in access time and utilization dramatically outweighs those cost considerations. How much would it cost to increase the floor space and hardware to create a similar increase in access time?

20) Learning is best served by adapting new technologies to match local needs and circumstances. Such adaptation requires the development of a thoughtful cohort of district "technology wizards" who represent the various perspectives of poets, historians, scientists, and others who will honor the educational philosophies of the

school while searching for the optimal applications of new technologies. Technology packages imported from the outside should be adopted only with scepticism and the intention of making significant modifications. Too often, packages are acquired because they relieve the district of responsibility for invention and adaptation.

CONCLUSION

If you have the good fortune of designing new spaces for technologies, make certain that you allow form to follow function. Avoid the boxed-in thinking of most planners of educational space. Give the school of the next century a chance to emerge from your own dreams and visions. Read Stanley Davis' *Future Perfect* (1987). Allow your thinking to cut loose from the paradigms and limited perspectives of the past. Give these new technologies a chance to "strut their stuff." You and your students deserve nothing less.

CHAPTER TWELVE

RESTRUCTURING AND THE NEW TECHNOLOGIES: CONFLICT OR COMPATIBILITY?

The new technologies available to schools could prove to be essential elements in a restructuring process. They might just as easily prove to be serious obstacles or distractions. Restructuring has been defined variously by different groups; thus much depends on the particular hopes, dreams, or apprehensions of each person. This also is true of the different technologies that are selected for the restructuring process.

THE CART BEFORE THE HORSE AGAIN!

Time and again we make change in schools by buying some flashy new cart, tying on some horses, providing a half-day of training, pointing the new cart down a very steep hill, giving it a shove, issuing a glowing press release, closing our eyes, and crossing our fingers as the wheels roll and the horses scream.

Is it any surprise that so little change ever seems to stick? We lurch from bandwagon to bandwagon as closets fill with yesterday's broken carts and faculty rooms fill with wounded horses. When we ask if restructuring requires new technologies, are we once more placing the cart before the horse?

We are doing so if we fail to consider which new technologies are basic to citizenship and problem-solving in an Age of Information, if we purchase technologies to perform smokestack tasks, or if we buy first and think last.

Mastery of new technologies, especially mastery of *information technologies,* is fundamental for young people who will do their problem-solving, voting, loving, and living in the next millenium. Any school that fails to blend mastery of technology throughout the curriculum is failing to achieve its fundamental mission at a very basic level. However, as Neil Postman argues in *Technopoly: the Surrender of Culture to Technology* (1992), any school that buys technology without careful consideration endangers its students; and Postman warns that such an uncritical embrace of technology is "a form of cultural AIDS" (p. 63).

TECHNOLOGY AS CULTURAL AIDS

Just what does Postman mean? *Technopoly* is a stage of civilization during which technology undermines much of the basis of human connectedness. Traditional beliefs and institutions crumble and finally collapse in the face of what Postman calls information glut and information chaos. Making meaning is subverted by a tidal wave of information. *Technopoly* then imposes its own belief system, "by redefining what we mean by religion, by art, by family, by politics, by history, by truth, by privacy, by intelligence, so that our definitions fit its new requirements. *Technopoly*, in other words, is totalitarian technocracy" (p. 48). According to Postman, *Technopoly* destroys the essential narratives of a culture, those myths and belief systems that make us human.

In *Technopoly,* people must find meanings in machines, technique, and scientism. Postman sees the process as subtle, insidious, and largely unnoticed. For example, an advertisement urges us to "Reach out and touch someone!" and yet few notice how *Technopoly* has distorted the meaning of the word "touch" to replace real touching with an electronic substitute. *Technopoly* even offers "virtual reality," an electronic out-of-body substitute for real world experience. When will *Technopoly* offer virtual schooling? And at what price? Or is it here already?

THE ANTIDOTE: TECHNOLOGY IN THE SERVICE OF HUMANKIND

If we carefully weigh the impact of each new technology prior to embracing it, we can better avoid the painful side-effects of infatuation and infection. We can select those technologies with the greatest likelihood of enhancing human togetherness. We can introduce those technologies in ways that improve communication, add to the power of human creation, and increase warmth, rather than isolate, insulate, and chill the users. We can go with technology that is "high touch" and "user friendly." We can practice "safe technology."

THE CURATIVE: TECHNOLOGY AS PURGATIVE

Those who would restructure schools come at the task with vastly different motives. Some leaders from institutions outside of schools bring relatively narrow agendas to the task. They have no lofty social goals; many of them would be satisfied with the capable worker. Here we find the emphasis upon world markets, global competition and workforce basics.

Elliott Eisner has done a fine job of critiquing their limited curriculum (1991). Little attention is devoted to citizenship, cooperation, the arts, or any of the character development that would make this country truly kinder and gentler. This group is intent on raising the productivity of America, intent on the bottom line, focused on the child as worker.

Those who see children as workers are quick to jump on *technology as teacher*, opting for applications that substitute machines for teachers. Holding generally low opinions of teachers, they see technology as "teacher proof." The teacher steps into the background, becoming machine "operative," while artificial intelligence takes over the task of feeding children lessons and rewards.

These are the same folk who use the word "restructuring" to replace "layoffs." Mean and lean. They love terms such as "right-sizing." They jump at "voice mail" as a way to channel telephone communications efficiently and inexpensively.

Fortunately, many business leaders are far more enlightened. Ameritech provides an excellent example of a school-business partnership in the Chicago area that stresses the networking, communication, and reasoning potentials of new technologies. Through the generous support of Ameritech and IBM, *Project Homeroom* provides hundreds of high school students, their parents, and their teachers an opportunity to communicate about learning over a Prodigy™ network.

IN THE AGE OF THE SMART MACHINE: INFORMATING VS. AUTOMATING

In *In the Age of the Smart Machine* (1988), Shoshana Zuboff of the Harvard Business School coined the term *informating* as an option to the prevalent business strategy of using information technologies to reduce human involvement in the work place (automating). After studying the introduction of such technologies in ten or more industries, Zuboff lamented the tendency to replace human decision-making with carefully programmed technologies and chronicled the negative social effects that one commentator has called "the electronic sweatshop" (Garson, 1988). In contrast, Zuboff noted the benefits arising from the attempts to elevate human decision-making as a result of the enhanced information supply and processing tools.

Leading studies of IT (information technology), such as that conducted by the MIT Sloan School of Management, suggest that IT is an essential strategy for "restructuring" business organizations to be more flexible and more responsive to customer preferences. In *The Corporation of the 1990s* (Morton, 1991), IT is viewed as essential for building what is called the "Networked Organization." The authors call for a radical shift in the culture of such organizations:

> *In a firm's efforts to change strategic market positioning, set strategy, or increase performance, the need to manage effectively the interdependence of subunits and people within the firm is increasingly recognized.*
>
> *The firm's ability to continuously improve the effectiveness of managing interdependence is the critical element in product, service or strategy innovations in the marketplace (the proactive dimension to strategy) and in effectively responding to new competitive threats (the reactive dimension). Networks, designed and enabled by information technology, are key to effectively managing this interdependency.*
>
> *Characteristics of the networked approach:*
> 1. *Shared goals*
> 2. *Shared expertise*
> 3. *Shared work*
> 4. *Shared decision-making*
> 5. *Shared timing and issue prioritization*
> 6. *Shared responsibility*
> 7. *Shared recognition and reward*

(Corporation of the 1990s, pages 192-93)

Schools undertaking restructuring can learn a great deal from corporations about the potential of IT for new visions of the society, the work place, and schooling. In *2020 Vision: Transforming Your Business Today to Succeed in Tomorrow's Economy,* Davis and Davidson claim that "Information enhancements have become the main avenue to revitalize mature businesses and to transform them into new ones" (p. 17).

To Speak with a Human, Touch "0"

While voice mail may bring us efficiency and cost savings, many good companies have decided not to use it to handle customer complaints or requests for assistance. Other companies, recognizing the frustration felt by the person forced to listen to long recordings with "no exit," have inserted exit instructions early in the message.

Schools face some of the same choices. Shall we automate or informate? Is a machine really more patient than a teacher, or simply less sensitive?

Clarifying the Mission

Schools must clarify what they are trying to do for young people. If they do not, if they allow smokestack paradigms to go unchallenged and unexamined, restructuring will pass and be forgotten.

Restructuring, then, should begin with a reconsideration of philosophy and belief systems. What is it we really believe about children and how they learn? Committees of educators, parents, students, and community members should spend time challenging the following beliefs:

1) Most children are too lazy to persist in a demanding task requiring much reading and thought.

2) Children of the TV generation require babysitting and entertainment. They cannot operate independently.

3) Our real job is custodial.

4) Parents are no longer doing their job.

5) Some kids (or types of kids) are not worth our time.

6) Most teachers prefer routine to adventure.

7) Change is the enemy.

8) It isn't fair to hold teachers responsible for student learning.

9) There always will be job security for teachers.

10) There always will be public schools.

11) People learn best by repetition.

12) It is our job to sort and sift students according to potential as early as possible.

13) Teachers can stop learning when they finish school.

14) Learning is something that happens in schools.

15) People learn best when they see a clear payoff.

16) People learn best in rectangular rooms listening to teachers explain things.

If these kinds of beliefs go unchallenged and unexamined, then it is unlikely that restructuring will proceed meaningfully, with or without new technologies. The belief systems will twist the new technologies to serve the old ways.

Witness the frequent mis-use of videodisc science programs which provide students with rich visual data that could lead to the development of student insight. Unless the teacher appreciates the value of students "making meaning," the videodisc player becomes a 1953 slide projector: The teacher shows picture after picture in sequence, explaining each to the class, much like any other slide show. Instead of asking open-ended questions that coax the class to convert data into insight, the teacher does the thinking for the class.

In a similar fashion, networks of computers tying teachers together across a vast school system can rapidly fall into the most pedestrian uses; data collection to serve "administrivia" or hierarchical control. Rather than reducing the isolation prevalent in most school systems by providing a new basis for community and the sharing of ideas, these new networks often serve more of a surveillance function.

WITHOUT INVESTING IN ADULT LEARNING, SIGNIFICANT CHANGE IS UNLIKELY

After reviewing a number of ambitious IT projects, the MIT Sloan study (Morton, 1991) concluded that most of them fell far short of expectations because they failed to invest sufficiently in the human resource development and cultural cultivation required to prepare employees to take full advantage of the new systems. Old ways were slow to respond to new opportunities and new technologies.

Unlike college professors, who are treated to many hours each week for research and exploration, the typical public school teacher is kept close to the "grindstone," working with children in a pressurized context that allows little time for reflection, research, discussion with other adults, or investigation. Innovative outcomes often emerge when groups of practitioners gather, but the culture of K-12 education does a great deal to suppress imagination and limit awareness. Restructuring is doomed from the beginning if participants have little opportunity to see what is possible.

School districts first should invest in developing a collaborative learning community. They should hold off on technology expenditures until those who are charged with the invention of new programs have had a chance to "see the world," as it were. Technology should be able to step outside and above the day-to-day survival activities of a school in order to see them with some perspective. They also need opportunities to see and ask questions about the challenges and goals that lie ahead.

Restructuring should begin with human-resource development, with cultivation of the human organization. The question of which technologies will best serve our students will seem far less perplexing when educators can rise above the smokestack verities and time-honored routines.

CHAPTER THIRTEEN

TALES OF HEROISM, WIZARDRY, AND COURAGE IN THE LIVES OF PARADIGM SHIFTERS

The challenges facing school leaders today require heroic action. To accomplish this feat, they must ally themselves with other heroes, such as staff developers, technology wizards, principals, teachers, and assistant superintendents who share their vision. Together they will set off on a journey marked by trials, tests, tribulations, and if all goes well, triumph.

The monster these heroes must fight is smokestack education: classroom instruction that emphasizes routine, compliance, memorization, lower-level thinking, and teacher domination. The society and the economy of the next decade require brainworkers and independent problem-solvers capable of inventing fresh approaches with which to respond to a rapidly changing world. But smokestack education leaves America ill equipped to compete in an increasingly high-tech, information-based, global economy; and it impedes the development of a healthy society, the "kinder and gentler" world once promised by President Bush.

This sacrifice of youthful talent must stop. In the Greek myth, Athens was required to sacrifice seven maidens and seven young men each year to appease the Minotaur. We sacrifice far more each year. The NAEP reports that fewer than

10% of our eleventh graders (still in school) are capable of performing tasks requiring high levels of reasoning power, the very kinds of thinking our society needs in order to thrive (Jones, et. al.,1992). Across the land, far too many of our students spend each morning wading through a dozen ditto sheets, filling in blanks, and practicing scripts.

THE IMPORTANCE OF KNOWING THE SIX STAGES OF THE HERO'S JOURNEY

Modern educators must learn from the heroes of old, modeling their journeys after those who have passed before. If they are successful, they will raise a generation of students who are "everyday heroes," intent on using their insights to make this a better world.

Educators must become "everyday heroes," and they must help their students become everyday heroes. In simplest terms, an everyday hero is a person who employs creative powers and energies to try to make life better for the community. Joseph Campbell (1988) describes a hero as "someone who has given his or her life to something bigger than oneself" (p. 123). Catford and Ray's *The Path of the Everyday Hero* (1991) is a great source for those who would like to learn more about this concept.

By studying the heroes of old, we can learn what to expect and be better prepared for the trials when they appear. Ignorance is the hero's greatest enemy; it allows fear and panic to undermine will and commitment at some crucial stage of the journey. We need to know, for example, that the hero almost always is tested on something that is a weakness. Lancelot's failure to reach the Holy Grail came not from failure to face other knights or dragons; armed combat was his strength. It was his inability to maintain vows of chastity that blocked him from the Grail. His biggest challenge was temptation, and his biggest enemy was himself.

Another problem heroes often faced in legends was *hubris,* excessive pride or arrogance. Hubris has been known to plague school leaders on occasion. The knowledge of such heroic perils can help the school leader to avoid repeating those mistakes.

We have paid too little attention to the very real risks facing those who would lead change efforts. We have done little to prepare leaders for those risks or equip them with the skills and courage required to stick with the journey.

By and large, the literature and research on educational change has been too rational, too logical, and too dispassionate. Not only have administrative training programs done little to encourage those who must undertake heroes' journeys, they have tended to promote a kind of status quo leadership style that has contributed to our present frozen condition.

Despite the warnings and the dangers, the educational hero heeds the call to adventure and steps forward on the path to a new and better educational future. She or he breaks through the paradigms, mind-sets, and myths that have long blocked progress. These educational heroes ask how schooling might change for the better.

1. INNOCENCE

According to Catford and Ray, there is a prelude to most journeys, a time during which all seems right with the world and the status quo seems acceptable (1991, p. 38). This time of innocence is the first stage of the hero's journey. But good teachers actually experience little of this steady-state in their careers because they are almost always dissatisfied with the results of their efforts. They are always searching for more effective ways to reach their classes.

Good teachers help others to explore the edges of their understanding. Thus these teachers spend much of their time with "negative space," the darkness we associate with the unknown. Because students promise a daily diet of surprise and emotion, teachers' attempts to establish reliable routines and practices are doomed from the outset. While that does not stop some teachers from trying, the best teachers recognize that learning should be an adventure for all, teachers and students alike. They recognize that learning is, almost by definition, a hero's journey and that innocence cannot long survive if learning is taking place.

2. The Call to Adventure

For the good teacher, the call to education is the beginning of the hero's journey. The call to adventure is the second stage.

If you are wondering whether you are experiencing the call, check your gut and ask if you feel risk gathering there. Check to see if your stress and anxiety levels have risen suddenly. Ask if there is some big decision to be made.

1. Are you feeling "out ahead" of the pack?

2. Are you isolated?

3. Do you feel that you see things differently suddenly?

4. Are you uneasy about repeating patterns you have long taken for granted?

5. Are you beginning to have more questions than answers?

6. Do the questions stay with you, demanding attention?

7. Is your dream life (while driving, running, showering, daydreaming or night dreaming) more turbulent?

If you answered many of these questions with a "yes," chances are that you are experiencing the call.

3. INITIATION

Once the journey has begun, the hero is sorely tested and nearly discouraged early on. This is in part because the hero is usually unclear regarding the true nature of the journey. Arrogance blocks understanding and learning. The very things we are sure we know are often the perceptions which block us from new truths. Almost always, the hero must experience disappointment, frustration, and near failure to achieve transformation and transcendence. The old skills must prove insufficient to meet the new challenges before the hero can acknowledge the need for new insight.

In most hero stories, there is a moment of despair when the hero is about to give up and lose heart. At these times, the hero often surrenders to some higher spiritual power, gives up control, stops fighting so hard, and suddenly acquires new powers and vision resulting from this surrender and openness.

In *The Art of the Long View,* Schwartz (1991) teaches scenario building as a way to prepare for an uncertain future. Basic to the art of scenario building is re-perceiving the world, laying aside assumptions and mind-sets that block our ability to see possibilities.

It is this kind of scenario-building that allowed Shell Oil —back in 1983, prior to Gorbachev's rise to power—to anticipate the break-up of the USSR. Shell Oil briefed the CIA on this scenario, but the CIA scoffed at the idea and refused to give it serious consideration. As a result, when the actual break-up occurred, the CIA was left unprepared. But Shell Oil was prepared for the "discontinuous" change, which thinkers like Drucker (1992) and Davis (1987) keep warning us about. In a similar fashion, school leaders are sometimes slow to let go of mind-sets that block future possibilities.

One thing we can learn from other heroes is that at the outset of the journey, we cannot be sure what it is we will need to discard and what it is that will lift us beyond the limitations of our past views. Most likely we will need to surrender ourselves to the learning process with open minds, trusting the process to show us the way. Often we find more answers as we enter the next stage, achieving major new insights with the help and synergism of allies.

4. ALLIES

In many myths, it is at the moment of surrender that allies suddenly appear to provide the hero with new wisdom, new perception, new tools, and new magic. It is almost as if one must be relieved of one's long-held illusions before one can be open to new insights.

Who are the allies one can count upon to provide the magic and the new perception? The educational hero may find allies where she or he least expects them. It may be a parent with unusual experience in the creation of music with new technologies, or it may be a local business person or religious leader. It may be a classroom teacher who has the same quest.

There is nothing wrong with searching out sages and professional consultants, but the hero is often apt to find truth in unusual quarters. It is more important to be open to new sources than it is to conduct some kind of fervent search. The danger of the fervent search is the likelihood that we inadvertently will seek those who confirm our wrong mind-sets.

5. BREAKTHROUGH

Breakthrough occurs when the hero applies new wisdom and perception to develop a novel approach. Insight fuels invention. There is a creative leap, the "Aha!" What passed for understanding in the past drops away like an old skin as new ideas emerge with the brilliance of a butterfly taking flight from its cocoon.

For the technology wizard, this might be the moment when a design team emerges from months of struggle and debate with a vision of a new technology lab. For the educational hero, it may be the moment when he or she knows that this new lab will catapult students into a whole new realm of learning and team invention.

6. CELEBRATION

Months later, the facility opens, students file in, and the design team stands back smiling, recognizing what they already knew. The new space is different from any they have seen in a school, but it is humming. The pieces of their dream have come together with the magic harmony of a symphony.

The celebration stage comes when a hero shares insight with the world or community, thereby enhancing the quality of life in some way. Great ideas become realities. Dreams become programs. Truths are revealed in actions.

It is not enough for the hero to grow and learn alone. The community must gain from the journey. The hero must share. Sharing permits transcendence.

THE HERO AS CREATOR

Catford and Ray (1991, pp. 24-27) draw a close parallel between the stages of the hero's journey and the six stages of the creative process:

> Preparation
>
> Frustration
>
> Incubation
>
> Strategizing
>
> Illumination
>
> Verification

In order to be successful during these six stages, they maintain that a creative hero needs the following four "magic" tools:

1) HAVING FAITH IN YOUR CREATIVITY

Because the journey will plunge you into darkness at various times, faith becomes essential. During those long trials, as answers and solutions prove evasive, the creative hero must believe in perseverance, that clarity will emerge eventually, that answers will, indeed, arise out of confusion and darkness. A lack of faith translates into a lack of courage and a tendency to play it safe, sticking with what is familiar and reassuring.

2) SUSPENDING NEGATIVE JUDGMENT

Because negative judgments virtually shut down creative production, the creative hero drives away doubt and criticism, especially during the exploration and idea-generation stages. The goal is to open one's mind to possibilities never before considered. If you find a judge perched on your shoulder and critiquing every new thought, banish him and invite your clown to takes its place. This is a time for playful consideration of intriguing futures.

3) PRACTICING PRECISE OBSERVATION

A visit to unfamiliar territory places a premium on careful observation. One cannot rely on previous experience and knowledge for guidance. The creative hero slows down activity, emphasizes reflection, and seeks understanding.

4) ASKING PENETRATING QUESTIONS

Precise observation relies on penetrating questions. Good questions are the tools we use to develop insight when encountering new and strange environments or experiences. Questions bring us out of the darkness and into the light. They probe negative space and help us to make meaning.

Questions are paradigm-busters. They challenge mind-sets. They "dis-illusion" us by undermining archaic myths. They free us by enabling a re-perceiving of potentiality. Questioning sets us free.

RELEVANCE FOR STUDENTS

Our students need these same four tools if they are to greet the new century as heroes. But the task of emphasizing student creativity, observation, and questioning will require a massive paradigm shift. Research on student questions indicates that the current ratio is 38 teacher questions for every 1 student question (Hyman, 1980). We have a very long way to go before we make student inquiry the prevailing practice.

We have come full circle back to the need to emphasize the kinds of thinking Toffler stresses in *Powershift* (1991). If we wish this generation of students to leave school as everyday heroes capable of tackling complicated and surprising problems imaginatively and resourcefully, we have a great deal of work to do.

ENCOURAGING THE HEROES

Paradigm shifters, according to Barker and most observers of the change process, often experience punishment, pain, doubt, and banishment. Instead of being greeted with open arms as heroes, they often are shunned, ignored, pilloried, or ostracized. They are labeled as heretics. The costs of challenging old paradigms are so high that conventional wisdom and self-preservation argue for silence.

If we expect significant change to take place in schools, we must find ways to support the questioners, the paradigm shifters, and the inventors who are willing to propose new scenarios and possibilities. Until we do a better job of removing barriers and penalties for this kind of thinking and action within the public schools, we are likely to see nothing more than incremental changes or first-order change—mere tinkering that does not go to the heart of the challenge.

If we do not do this, second-order, fundamental, and discontinuous change may arrive from the outside as free market forces approach the challenge with far fewer reservations and far less baggage.

CHAPTER FOURTEEN

FLEXADIGM, DON'T PARADIGM!

We do not need to replace the old paradigm with a new paradigm. What we need is a *flexadigm*. A *flexadigm* is a quiver of paradigms! In suggesting that old paradigms must give way to new paradigms (Barker, 1992), we still are caught in an old way of thinking, which assumes we move from one plateau to another, replacing one system with another.

WHY FLEXADIGM?

One of the many synonyms for paradigm, "mind-set," helps to clarify the problem. What we need are open minds, not closed ones. We cannot afford operating procedures, rules, and attitudes that are "set." They must stay flexible and responsive. They must be tentative and experimental. They must be open to question.

No paradigm will meet the challenges and needs of a turbulent, quickly changing world. We need a collection of operating procedures that will allow us to respond flexibly and dynamically. A flexadigm is somewhat like a quiver of paradigms because we can reach in and select the approach which fits the circumstances. Without a flexadigm, we may become paradigm prisoners.

111

Instead of being able to rely on standard operating procedures—paradigms we can count on to direct our energies productively and effectively—we find ourselves forced to muddle about, experiment, and engage in continuous learning or adjustment. Just about the time we see how to handle some new technology like the Apple IIGS, the school district goes out and buys a batch of IBMs or Macs, which require a whole new round of skill development and adaptation.

Sometimes when districts launch innovations, staff will ask, "When will things return to normal?" But we must consider the possibility that normality is itself a phenomenon of the past, a by-product of a relatively stable industrial society. If present social and economic trends persist, normality may never return.

How do flexadigms work?

The employee of the next decade will possess a change ethic, an attitude that welcomes change, applies skill to its management, and views its impact on others compassionately. This person will have an array of change strategies and a collection of flexible operating procedures—a flexadigm—from which to select a fitting response to a particular challenge or situation.

In the field of education, Bruce Joyce has proposed an instructional flexadigm in his approach to teachers as expert instructors drawing from multiple models of instruction, a repertoire of techniques from which the teacher selects a strategy to fit a particular student or class situation (Joyce, 1988). It may be "Jigsaw" from cooperative learning, or it may be guided practice; the teacher exercises judgement. There can be no reliance on simple recipes or routines. The teacher mixes and matches, meeting the surprises, adjusting, modifying and adapting, constantly observing and reflecting to see how the lesson might be made more successful.

IMPLICATIONS FOR SCHOOLS?

To replace the notion of a new paradigm with the notion of a flexadigm is itself a dramatic paradigm shift for schools, one with significant implications for planning and organizational development.

- *Staff Recruitment*—Forecasters predict a major turnover in the teaching staff during this decade. Districts may wish to re-evaluate staff-recruitment paradigms. How can you identify new staff who will possess and maintain a change ethic? Districts would be wise to avoid those with excessive needs for stability in favor of those with a taste for change and innovation.

- *Organizational Development*—Considering the reality that many existing staff members will stay with the district well into the next century, the district may wish to blend cultural goals into the staff-development plan. Peter Senge's *Fifth Discipline: The Art and Practice of the Learning Organization* (1990) provides an excellent model. He suggests strategies to empower all employees to question how to improve performance and modify procedures on a daily basis.

- *Student Learning Outcomes*—If employers expect to see graduates possessing a *change ethic*, we must ask how we can provide students with learning experiences that engender such an attitude, as well as a repertoire of skills. This task will require a fresh look at the ways students spend their time. A curriculum must become more than a list of topics and concepts. The kinds of experiences and teaching strategies required to achieve the attitudinal and skill goals also must be identified. That list, in turn, may have implications for staff development programs. Program assessment must move from measurement of factual learning to embrace such

113

issues as student attitudes and skills as applied to realistic life situations.

CONCLUSION

Times are changing, and schools must move from the trailing edge of society to the leading edge by grasping the excitement implicit in the adventure associated with open-minded, flexible operations. We must move past the notion of finding a new paradigm, as if there is some Grail waiting to be discovered. Instead, we must recognize that the turbulence and discontinuous change of the Information Age require schools to practice and model flexadigms.

CHAPTER FIFTEEN

THE COMFORT ZONE, RISKS, AND CHANGE

INTRODUCTION: THE COMFORT ZONE DEFINED

We are all, to some extent, creatures of habit. We rely on and trust routines to guide many of our actions and decisions. We often seek manuals or guides to "show us the way." Much like deer returning to a favorite water hole, we have our cherished pathways and traditions. These habits, routines, guides, pathways, and traditions combine with beliefs to create a culture, a way of living that serves the very desirable purpose of pulling us together.

Much of our adult life is devoted to the development of reliable routines and habits that will operate smoothly and predictably to produce the outcomes we seek. We seek to figure out the system. We are careful about rocking the boat, lest we spill wind from the sails and lose head way. We become expert; we know what we are doing. The rules are clear.

In times of rapid change and turbulence, what worked yesterday may not work today. In such times, the *comfort zone* is much like the sand into which the ostrich sticks its head. The comfort zone is the leading cause of what Joel Barker (1992) would call "paradigm paralysis" and what Argyris calls "skilled incompetence" (Senge, 1990).

Not every Colonist wished to travel across the Appalachians to see what kind of land lay on the other side. Many—in fact, the majority—preferred the safety and predictability of the settled coastline. Most, it turns out, preferred the *comfort zone.* A few hardy women and men, probably considered "fool-hardy" by their peers, were curious and hungry enough to brave the hardships, the angry native populations, and the uncharted wilderness in exchange for freedom, opportunity, and adventure. During these years, "adventurer" was not a term of endearment. It implied a degree of recklessness and a disregard for rules and boundary lines.

Even today, the word "adventure" connotes irresponsibility, as the following thesaurus-generated list illustrates: antic, caper, escapade, joke, lark, mischief, prank, and trick.

In *Moby Dick,* Melville, speaking through his character, Ishmael, divided the world into those who would remain ashore and those who would brave the ocean, suggesting that the latter group was somehow more noble. But the ending of the story provides little encouragement for those who would venture far from a comfortable harbor. Ishmael barely survived. The crew drowned. The hunt for Moby Dick led to death and ruin.

The message of *Moby Dick* is filled with paradox and ambiguity. If one stays safely inland or anchored behind the breakwater, one is condemned to lead an ignoble life. If, on the other hand, one sails out into the ocean in search of a bolder, grander destiny, one faces the likelihood of extinction. We are damned if we do, and we are damned if we don't. The *comfort zone,* then, is both trap and refuge; and each organization— whether it be a hospital, a school, a computer company, or the U.S. Marines—must make astute judgments about when to head for the open seas and when to rest at anchor.

The Comfort Zone and School Restructuring

Unfortunately, life in the comfort zone is addictive. Once we have tasted the security and predictability of life in the comfort zone, our desire for comfort often seems to grow; and we require ever-larger doses to maintain the habit. We begin to confuse the comfort zone and the feelings it generates with normality. Comfort is normal, we feel. Discomfort is abnormal. Risk is an enemy, because it threatens disruption. Adventure is a high-stakes gamble. Leadership is the ability to provide and maintain comfort, rather than the kind of influence once provided by whaling captains or wagon masters.

Schools are especially vulnerable to the phenomenon of the comfort zone, because so many people have done their best to make life uncomfortable for educators in recent decades. The constant babble of outside attacks and reform initiatives has inspired many school people to "circle the wagons" in order to protect the system. Our need for comfort probably is exaggerated because we have suffered frequent, intense criticism during a time when our jobs became especially challenging as the society and the nature of families dumped huge new responsibilities upon us.

The society has done little to provide schools with encouragement for innovative solutions. To the contrary, in many places, inventive educators have tasted the fate of Ahab's crew. Often the board of education that called for change is soon replaced by one elected to block their efforts. The inventive period of the late 1960s and 1970s included so many misguided ventures and mistakes that its memory still looms over this generation of teachers like the Great Depression loomed over our parent's heads. We remember those wildly exciting days when we pulled down walls and set children free. We also remember the executions and the walls going back up again. We saw many inventive teachers leave the life of adventure behind, laying down their chalk to pick up new careers. These

117

institutional memories act to block change whenever wild-eyed reformers call on us to again pull down the walls of tradition.

All too often, we speak of school restructuring as if it were a temporary move from one comfort zone to a new zone. It is something like remodeling a restaurant, we hope. We change the paint, bring in some new furniture, add a sound system; but we still cook and serve food when we re-open. After a week or two in the new surroundings, we fully expect to be "up to speed" and comfortable with the new routines. A popular metaphor accuses us of "rearranging the deck chairs on the Titanic."

The very choice of the word, "restructuring," to label what we are about is flawed, because it implies that we will trade in an old structure for a new one. It echoes models of change from the 1960s, which spoke of "unfreezing" an organization prior to the development of new operating procedures, which, once fully tested and successful, could be "frozen" in place.

In Chapter 14 I argued that organizations will need to remain flexible and responsive during the next decade, selecting operating procedures and responses to problems from a "quiver of paradigms." One danger lurking behind the "restructuring" movement is the implicit (probably false) promise that things will return to normal after several years of meetings, training, and change. The return to normal and a high level of comfort actually can emerge as a major goal of a team. Premature freezing back into almost any single new set of operating procedures will leave the system insufficiently responsive and adaptable to adjust to what will continue to be changing conditions.

A second danger hiding within the restructuring movement is the possibility that adult comfort needs will inhibit innovative planning. An example would be the request by a planning team that computer specialists be hired to show students in elementary schools how to use new technologies in a

118

lab setting. While this suggestion is usually defended by emphasizing the advantages of expertise, the strategy may absolve regular teachers from responsibility and protect them from venturing out of the comfort zone. But if those teachers join the students in learning from the specialist, it may be an excellent way for them to explore unfamiliar territory.

Even though the gap between what most schools are doing for students today and what the society needs them to be doing is growing wider, tinkering and first-order change is still the norm. As is true with many addictions, we express denial and are angry that the outsiders show little understanding of the burdens that arrive each day on our doorsteps. Studies show that most schools have failed to integrate the use of new technologies into math, social studies, English, and science classes and that we remain on the "trailing edge" of the society with regard to technology. But we keep repeating the same technology planning procedures, which place hardware above philosophy, isolate the pioneer, and protect the reluctant. Cuban (1992) offers a somewhat pessimistic forecast, suggesting that technology is most likely to catch on when it is used to fit the old operating procedures.

THE COMFORT ZONE AND STUDENT-CENTERED LEARNING

One of the most intriguing efforts to explore the potential of new technologies to alter the ways that students learn and think is the The Systems Thinking and Curriculum Innovation Network Project (STACI^N), developed by Ellen Mandinach and her team at ETS. This project has been exploring the use of a software program called STELLA™, a simulation-modeling package, for six years with six high schools and two middle schools.

STELLA™ can lead students progressively through four levels of systems thinking. For example, it can begin with testing the consequences of changing parameters in a computer simulation of a wolf eco-system. Mandinach (1992, p. 14) identifies four levels of systems thinking proceeding from *parameter manipulation* to the construction of simplified models, called *constrained modeling,* and then to the development of more complex models, called *epitome modeling,* and finally, to the creation of *learning environments.* The higher up this ladder the student proceeds, the greater the understanding.

Systems thinking is a high priority in both the new NCTM standards (Frye, 1989) and Project 2061 (AAAS, 1989), pioneering efforts to change the teaching of math and science to meet our needs for the next century. But despite careful planning, a well-designed training program, and a very thoughtful implementation strategy, the researchers candidly report that the introduction of systems thinking with STACI[N] has taken a long time, has required patience, and has worked best with teachers who are able to tolerate a high degree of student control and surprise (Mandinach, 1992).

Mandinach goes into considerable detail relating the various stages of teacher adaptation to new technologies:

> *We have observed that some teachers need to be completely knowledgeable about and feel confident of their mastery of the systems thinking approach in order to use it effectively. However, basic knowledge and confidence are not sufficient conditions to insure success in implementing the systems approach. The teachers must be willing and able to share control of the classroom and learning process with the students. With traditional methods, teachers most often know what sorts of questions and responses students are likely to pose. Teachers therefore can impart knowledge and exercise control through their disciplinary expertise.*

> *However with the systems thinking approach, these interactions change substantially. Because there are generally many solution paths with the systems*

approach, there is no way that a teacher can anticipate the range of questions and possible solutions students might suggest. As the innovative technology (both theory and equipment) become a more prominent part of the classroom, the teacher no longer serves as the sole expert with absolute mastery and control of content knowledge and instructional procedures. Instead, learning becomes more interactive with responsibility shared among teachers and students. The teachers no longer function solely as transmitters of content knowledge. Instead, they become facilitators of learning. Students play a more active role in their own learning. The shift often requires teachers to take risks and develop new instructional strategies to facilitate the learning process. They must relinquish deeply entrenched pedagogical behaviors. This creates some fundamental shifts in the way classrooms, teachers and students function. Not all teachers are capable of or willing to explore or accept this evolving role. (pp. 10-11)

Mandinach goes beyond the ACOT stages to add a fourth one, the *innovation* stage, in which a teacher goes well beyond "the mandated scope of the curriculum toward a complete restructuring of teaching and learning activities" (p. 13).

Regrettably, the STACI[N] experience bolsters Cuban's pessimistic forecast (1992) for the chances of a fundamental shift in the use of technologies for schools. The paragraphs quoted above echo the theme of this article, which suggests that adult comfort needs often stand in the way of learning, pioneering and innovation.

We are left with a real quandary. If we determine that this generation of students needs to be educated by "a guide on the side, not a sage on the stage," what do we do with all the sages who refuse to be guides? We have excellent models at hand from such researchers as Mandinach to guide willing teachers *comfortably* from one stage to another *if they are willing,* but we have not confronted the challenge of those who cannot tolerate any change.

CHAPTER SIXTEEN

JUDGING THE SUCCESS OF NEW TECHNOLOGIES

In the past dozen years, little progress has been made toward judging the success of new technologies. Why is this so? How do we explain the enormous commitment of dollars to technologies with so little evidence available as to determine their benefits?

Test out your own district's commitment to careful planning and program evaluation by completing the District Technology Self-Assessment Form on pages 134-140 of this chapter. Ask colleagues to share their perceptions. Which issues need the most attention?

THE IMPORTANCE OF PROGRAM EVALUATION

We need to know more about the effects of new technologies on the learning of students in order to support the thoughtful selection of technologies, the design and implementation of new programs, and the marketing of new technologies to various school constituencies.

SELECTION OF TECHNOLOGIES

Given a limited hardware budget, what kind of investment will pay the greatest learning dividends? In order to answer that question, the district must first clarify its own objectives. What are the desired student outcomes? Is the district looking

123

to equip students with job-related technology skills, such as database research, writing, graphics and group-problem-solving? Or is the improvement of reading scores a higher priority? Once the district determines its priority, it should be able to turn to research on the relative merits of various platforms and systems in comparison with other educational delivery systems that are not technology-based. Unfortunately, because there are few studies that provide such comparative data, many districts have only the data supplied by vendors when shopping for technology.

PROGRAM DESIGN AND IMPLEMENTATION

What you don't know can hurt you. Schools need frequent and skillful data collection in order to modify and adapt newly implemented programs. It is the responsibility of district technology planning committees to identify research questions worth asking, commission an evaluation design, and explore the significance of findings on a frequent basis, suggesting program changes as data warrant them.

It makes great sense to learn from the experience and mistakes of others instead of re-inventing the wheel, yet the literature on technology programs is often "testimonial" in character, meaning that a district pioneer is writing an article describing the benefits of a particular innovation. These articles tend to minimize the difficulties and exaggerate the benefits of the innovation. They also rarely include reliable data, which might provide clues for program designers in other districts to decide which elements to adopt and which ones to avoid.

Formative evaluation—the collection of data as a program proceeds in order to learn enough to guide adaptation of the program—is of prime importance. The implementation team keeps asking important questions and collecting relevant data, some of which will be quantitative (numerical) and some of which will be qualitative (descriptive). The goal is reflective practice, continually asking "What's happening? How might we change what we are doing to improve results?" Programs must be implemented with an experimental spirit and style, assuming that the assumptions and ideas that guided the original design will deserve reconsideration as implementation proceeds.

Data collection often is viewed with suspicion by staff members, who worry that the data might be used to evaluate their own performance. The mere hint of accountability causes defensiveness in many districts. In order to avoid such a reaction, staff members must have a strong voice in the design of the study and the collection of the data. They need to receive appropriate training in formative evaluation, so that they can see the benefits of data collection for program adjustment and development. Teachers, if they are to act as technology pioneers, must become researchers, applying new technologies to learning challenges with an eye toward testing hypotheses and developing successful strategies.

Even good programs, like bushes and trees, can benefit from careful and timely pruning. In conjunction with research data, the program team keeps asking what changes need to be made in the original plan. What elements should be eliminated, cut back, and modified?

Summative evaluation—the collection of data to judge the overall success of a program—is also important to help district decision-makers determine the return on investment. The district needs to know how much bang it bought with its buck. When boards of education pay for elaborate systems and nobody can tell them the "return on investment" three years later, they often become suspicious, doubtful, and uncooperative about new ventures.

Marketing New Technologies

Because many school district constituencies, such as senior citizens and parents, did not use these new technologies during their own schooling, the support for such programs is often quite soft, especially in recessionary times when budgets are tight. Because anything viewed as innovative is vulnerable to the budget ax, school districts would be wise to involve all constituencies in seeing and experiencing the benefits of these new technologies. Marketing involves getting to know the needs and interests of all the groups and then opening school technology programs to community participation in order to engender feelings of ownership and support.

Evaluation reports can be an important element in these marketing campaigns. How has student writing changed because of the writing labs? What proof can you provide that student performance has changed dramatically for the good? What does the new technology offer that the old technologies could not match?

Because few school districts invest in such data collection for new technologies and the programs associated with them, they rob themselves of several important opportunities. The data play an important role in building a successful program, and they can be helpful in winning community support. Without data to show student outcomes, new technologies can too easily be characterized as frills.

Unfortunately, in too many cases, the hardware and the technology are seen as the program itself. First we buy the equipment and then we ask how we might use it. Evaluation is not even an after-thought.

THE SAD STATE OF RESEARCH ON TECHNOLOGY PROGRAMS

As the table reproduced on page 127 demonstrates, the number of articles on evaluation of K-12 educational technology has never exceeded 40. And many of those do not report actual findings but explore the issue of evaluation. Furthermore, according to Becker (1988), many of the published program evaluations are seriously flawed.

Number of Evaluation of K-12 Educational Technology Articles Reported by ERIC Each Year 1980-92

1980: 8   1981: 16   1982: 10   1983: 29   1984: 25

1985: 22   1986: 32   1987: 27   1988: 27   1989: 27

1990: 29   1991: 36   1992: 7

One of the most important questions for further research, posed by Becker and others back in 1988, was the relative effectiveness of CAI versus other expenditures, such as tutoring or staff development to improve teachers' reading or math instruction. This question remains poorly addressed.

Fortunately, there are several large county systems, cities, and think tanks, such as Research for Better Schools, that have invested in meaningful program evaluations with considerable reliability and validity.

Examples of Effective Research

Writing to Read

One example of effective evaluation is the series of reports available from the New York City Public Schools evaluating the IBM *Writing to Read* program over several years. These studies establish control groups, have sound design standards, and report findings in a comprehensive fashion. A district considering purchase and implementation of this program could learn a great deal about what kinds of learner outcomes one could expect from the investment; but one must be careful to read beyond the abstract of such studies, because the summaries often mask or fail to report important findings.

The abstract below fails to mention, for example, that the impact of *WTR* on writing performance, compared with the performance of non-*WTR* students, was strongest in first grade but virtually disappeared in third grade. The hypothesis is that the regular first-grade programs traditionally pay less attention to writing, while writing instruction is important in traditional third-grade programs. This suggests that the achievement gains in first grade that were associated with *WTR* may have been replicated by teaching writing more frequently in the traditional first-grade classes.

WRITING TO READ 1988-89. EVALUATION SECTION REPORT.

The Writing to Read Program (WTR) objectives for 1988-89 included: to extend and support the implementation of the WTR program in New York City elementary schools; to promote the reading and writing achievement of kindergarten, first-, and second-grade students; and to introduce students in early childhood to computer technology. In 1988-89 the program served 87 schools in 22 community school districts. The methods used to evaluate the program included on-site interviews, lab and classroom observations, questionnaires distributed to all program participants and a selected group of parents, pre- and post-program writing samples, and reading achievement scores for the Metropolitan Achievement Test for both selected program participants and matching control groups. Overall reaction to the program was positive. Most participants believed that the program provided a good foundation in basic skills, helped to develop confident and mature writers, and that the computers and center setting were significant motivational devices. Some of the additional major findings included: (1) WTR program has little immediate impact, and no long-term impact on improving reading performance of participating students when compared with other reading programs; (2) students in the program made significant progress in their writing; (3) WTR students improved their writing skills to a greater degree than did similar students who did not participate in the program; and (4) monolingual students at the kindergarten level showed a statistically significant improvement in writing over bilingual kindergartners. (Eleven tables of data are included. One appendix includes the Writing Sample Scoring Scale.)

RESEARCH FOR BETTER SCHOOLS WRITING EVALUATION—DELAWARE

Collaborating with the Delaware Department of Instruction, Francine Beyer, a researcher with Research for Better Schools, tested the following three hypotheses regarding writing instruction combined with word processing at the middle-grade level:

- Student writing skills would be improved through the use of computer-assisted instruction for the teaching of the writing process.

- Student enjoyment of writing would be improved through the use of computer-assisted instruction for the teaching of the writing process.

- Student enjoyment of computer-assisted instruction for writing would be improved through the use of computer-assisted instruction for the teaching of the writing process. (p. 2)

This study was conducted in 16 schools, 13 of which provided reasonably comparable control groups. The researcher identified both process and outcome objectives of the project, noting that process objectives (how the program was delivered) must be met for findings regarding outcomes to be significant. This process data also would be used to adjust program implementation.

Districts wishing to construct local evaluations for writing programs may want to model their design after this excellent study, because it effectively combines formative with summative evaluation.

The study found that all three study hypotheses were supported by the evaluation data, as participants in experimental groups generally achieved greater gains in skill and attitude than did members of control groups.

Even such well designed evaluations and programs sometimes encounter some interesting design issues. Subtle though they may be, these issues deserve careful attention by those creating evaluations. In the RBS study, for example, growth in student writing skill was measured using writing samples that relied on paper and pencil rather than the new technology. How might the results have differed if experimental groups had been permitted to compose their samples on the word processor? If one believes that the word processor empowers a different kind of *idea processing* because of its low risk, flexible editing, and re-writing, how well will that growth show up if the student must revert to the old (paper and pencil) technology? It is a bit like testing the effect of new composite tennis rackets on a player's service by doing pre- and post-tests using wooden rackets.

Reading the study carefully, a second subtle but important issue emerges. During the year of this program, many of the students evidently composed their first drafts on paper and then transferred them to the computer. For those who prize the playfulness of composing on the computer, this behavior signals what may have been a fairly serious problem. What percentage of the students were able to actually perform pre-writing exercises and first drafts on the computers? Did access and time issues block many students from this experience? The study does not tell us; but the answers to the questions could prove instructive, as one might hypothesize that students would perform even more strongly if given such opportunities.

A third issue worth considering is the appropriateness of using a timed writing sample as a measure of student writing proficiency after spending a year on writing as a process, since this approach to writing emphasizes the importance of stretching writing out over time to allow for ideas to percolate. The instrument may not fit the program and may minimize differences between control groups and experimental groups, since writing samples play to the non-process, time-pressured approach to writing once typical of most school writing programs.

I offer these comments as a cautionary note to illustrate the peculiar challenge of designing valid evaluation studies for new technologies. Here we have an excellent study that should serve as a model, and yet the instrumentation available to us (such as pencil and paper, timed writing samples) may belong to an old paradigm unsuited to measuring the effects of various new technology programs. If we are not careful, these design issues may depress differences between experimental and control groups, eventually undermining support for the new programs.

Why So Little Technology Evaluation?

In this section we will explore a number of hypotheses that might explain the limited number of evaluation reports on technology. Following each hypothesis will appear a rationale, most of which will be conjecture.

Hypothesis #1: Most school districts do not have the expertise or the resources to conduct solid evaluation studies. Most of the existing studies have been completed by large districts, vendors, or universities. Few districts have personnel with formal evaluation skills or the specific assignment to conduct such evaluations, and research rarely is conducted as part of the decision-making process. The collection and analysis of data, a cornerstone in the Total Quality movement, is rare in many school districts. In times of scarce resources, these are the kinds of budgets and projects that are cut first.

Hypothesis #2: Program proponents have a vested interest in protecting new programs from scrutiny. Those who push new frontiers and encourage large expenditures are taking a considerable risk, especially when there is little reliable data available to predict success in advance. Careful program evaluation puts the innovation under a magnifying glass and increases the risk to the pioneers.

Hypothesis #3: Accountability sometimes runs counter to the culture of the school. Many school districts have been careful to avoid data collection that might be used to judge performance.

Hypothesis #4: There is little understanding of formative evaluation as program steering. Since most program evaluation in the past has been summative (Does it work?), few school leaders have much experience with using data formatively to steer programs and modify them. While this kind of data analysis would seem to be more useful, more helpful, and less threatening than summative evaluation, lack of familiarity may breed suspicion.

Hypothesis #5: Vendors have much to lose and little to gain from following valid research design standards. Districts are unlikely to pour hundreds of thousands of dollars into computers and software that will produce no significant gains. Careful research design tends to depress some of the bold results associated with gadgetry and the Hawthorne effect. Amazing first year gains, for example, often decline as programs enter their third year. In some cases, vendors report only the districts or schools with the best results and remain silent about those which are disappointing.

Hypothesis #6: School leaders have little respect for educational research. Many school leaders joke that you can find an educational study to prove or disprove the efficacy of just about any educational strategy. Studies have shown that such leaders typically consult little research as they plan educational programs.

Hypothesis #7: Technology is seen often as capital rather than program. Some school leaders do not associate technology with program. They view technology as equipment that does not require program evaluation. Equipment may be evaluated for speed, efficiency, and cost, but not for learning power.

Hypothesis #8: Evaluation requires clarity regarding program goals. Unless the district is clear about its learning objectives in terms that are observable and measurable, as was done in the RBS study, it will be difficult to design a meaningful evaluation study. In some districts, the technology is selected before a determination is made regarding its uses.

Hypothesis #9: Adherence to evaluation design standards may create political problems. In addition to increasing risk by spotlighting a program, evaluation also can anger parents, as some students are involved in experimental groups and others may have to put up with the traditional approach. Random selection can anger people on either side of the innovation, participating teachers included. Voluntary participation, on the other hand, immediately distorts the findings.

Hypothesis #10: Innovative programs are so demanding that launching an evaluation at the same time may overload the system. Many schools are perennially stable and conservative organizations with a preference for first-order change (tinkering) rather than second-order change (fundamental change). The need for stability conflicts with innovation. Because the potential for resistance runs high in such organizations, many leaders may forgo evaluation just to win the opportunity for a change.

CONCLUSION

We have devoted nearly a dozen years to exciting new technologies without penetrating most of the regular classroom programs or achieving the kind of program integration that makes sense. Much technology use is tangential. Before we can expect to see a greater infusion into the regular program areas, we must gather more convincing evidence regarding the learning effects of these technologies. Yet it seems unrealistic to expect that either vendors or school districts can be expected to fill this void during the next few years.

Perhaps it is time for our federal research dollars to tackle this challenge in a comprehensive, highly organized fashion. Meanwhile, we must muddle through, the blind leading the blind, trusting to our instincts and our intuition rather than solid data. Wise districts will keep an eye out for studies like the RBS/Delaware writing project reported in this article; and they will form local versions to test their computerized writing programs, borrowing research design and instruments from professionals in the field.

District Technology Self-Assessment Form

1. Is there a sense of purpose? a plan?

excellent (5)   good (4)   fair (3)   weak (2)   poor (1)

Related Questions: Is there a written district technology plan that clarifies philosophical commitments and directions for district staff? Does this plan focus on the horizon—the long view? Does it leave room for steering and flexibility as staff learns through experience? Does it address all critical elements of program implementation, including staff development as well as hardware purchases? Is the plan research-based? Were all key constituents involved in creating the plan?

2. Is the technology being used?

excellent (5)   good (4)   fair (3)   weak (2)   poor (1)

Related Questions: Does the district have some method to quantify or track the proportion of time that equipment is being used by students or community members? Is there a system to figure out which staff members are making use of the equipment and which are not? Does the administration and the Board take a position with regard to computer and technology usage? How much usage would be desirable? 100% of the school day? 75%? 65%? 35%? Is there a gap between desired and actual? Does anyone know why? Is there a staff plan to narrow the gap?

3. IS TECHNOLOGY BLENDED INTO REGULAR CLASSROOM LEARNING?

excellent (5)   good (4)   fair (3)   weak (2)   poor (1)

Related Questions: If technologies are basic tools for managing information in an Age of Information, they should be used broadly, within the art classrooms, the English classrooms, the vocational classrooms, and all others. Studies of schools have shown that technology use is often centered in special "niches" and departments, such as a computer department or the media center, and the use often is concentrated in the hands of a narrow group of pioneers or champions. Are appropriate uses of technologies written into all of the district curriculum documents as mandatory activities to prepare students for the next century? Do all subject teachers make use of on-line databases, CD-ROM discs, and wordprocessing for research projects? Do students learn to create multimedia reports? If your district uses CAI (computer-assisted instruction) or an ILS (integrated learning system) approach, how closely are those learning experiences dove-tailed with their corresponding subject areas? If a child is doing reading practice on the computer, will it be on the same skills as she or he is developing with the rest of the language arts program? Is the new technology an organ transplant that has been accepted, or is it a grafted limb being rejected?

4. DOES THE USE OF TECHNOLOGY MIRROR WORKPLACE REALITIES?

excellent (5)   good (4)   fair (3)   weak (2)   poor (1)

Related Questions: Has your district explored how adult workers currently are using technologies to do scientific research, write, plan, design, evaluate, etc.? Has that exploration been translated into school experiences and programs? Is technology thought of primarily as a teaching tool or as a problem-solving tool for everyday life? How well are the school technology experiences preparing students for the Information Age workplace? Is there an explicit district definition of the Information Age? Is staff aware of how the use of information is transforming work and the kinds of skills required by today's workers? Has Toffler's *Power Shift* (Chapter 3) been reviewed carefully? Was ASTD's *Workplace Basics* considered? Are technologically savvy representatives of the profit and non-profit sectors consulted when the district does technology planning?

5. IS THE STAFF ADEQUATELY PREPARED TO USE THE TECHNOLOGY?

excellent (5)   good (4)   fair (3)   weak (2)   poor (1)

Related Questions: Has the Board funded a comprehensive staff development plan over 3 to 5 years or more to provide all teachers with sufficient technology skills to implement an appropriate program? Are all teachers required to acquire such skills? Are assessment plans in place to determine what course offerings need to be added in future years? Does staff development take place during the regular work year and work day, or is it added on in ways that require teachers to subsidize the learning with volunteered time? Is compensation for training/learning reasonable and fair?

6. DOES THE STAFF EVER VISIT THE WORKPLACE?

excellent (5)   good (4)   fair (3)   weak (2)   poor (1)

Related Questions: What provisions are made for staff members to spend time in the modern workplace to see how technologies are employed? What percentage of English teachers, for example, have spent a day in a modern newspaper office, seeing how technologies support the writing, design, layout, and production of a newspaper? How many science teachers have visited a modern science lab to see how computers are used to conduct experiments and model scientific phenomena? How many media specialists have visited modern libraries offering cutting-edge information systems?

7. IS ACCESS TO TECHNOLOGY EQUITABLE?

excellent (5)   good (4)   fair (3)   weak (2)   poor (1)

Related Questions: Does the district monitor technology use by gender, race, location, and academic track to make certain that access is equitable? What kinds of data are collected and reported to help guarantee equal access? When evidence arises that there are gaps of various kinds, what provision is made to close such gaps?

8. WHAT KINDS OF RELATIONSHIPS DO STUDENTS HAVE WITH MACHINES?

excellent (5)   good (4)   fair (3)   weak (2)   poor (1)

Related Questions: Has the board and the professional staff explored community values about desirable relationships between students and machines? Are these values communicated explicitly in board policy or in a district technology plan? How much time should students be engaged with various kinds of technologies? Who should be in control, the student or the machine? What are the long-term consequences of such relationships? How do they relate to other educational goals, such as citizenship and self-esteem?

9. ARE IMPLICIT VALUES TAUGHT BY TECHNOLOGIES?

excellent (5)   good (4)   fair (3)   weak (2)   poor (1)

Related Questions: Is there a system in place to review the implicit values or hidden curriculum taught by various technologies? If computer software rewards students for correct responses by providing game time or opportunities to blow up aliens, for example, is such a reward system consistent with board policy and community values? Does the technology stress extrinsic or intrinsic rewards? Is responsibility for reviewing such issues clearly identified? Is there a board policy regarding software piracy and violations of copyright? Do students see ethical behavior modeled by the professional staff? Are ethical issues concerning technologies addressed by such curriculum areas as social studies? Are students taught critical-thinking and critical-viewing skills to equip them to counter propaganda and media distortions? Will they emerge from schooling as thoughtful consumers or impulsive consumers? Will they be passive viewers or active viewers?

10. Does the technology enhance self-esteem, independence and imagination?

excellent (5)　　good (4)　　fair (3)　　weak (2)　　poor (1)

Related Questions: Workplace Basics states the need for workers who know how to learn independently, come up with novel solutions to problems, and ride through the turbulence of a changing economy and society with self-confidence and adaptability. Are district technology experiences designed to deliver that kind of workforce? How do you assess progress toward such goals? Do you measure student self-esteem? independence? imagination? Is there a program review process to determine which learning experiences are most likely to promote the growth of such qualities?

11. Is the technology more effective than alternative strategies?

excellent (5)　　good (4)　　fair (3)　　weak (2)　　poor (1)

Related Questions: Is the technology the only way to provide a particular learning experience, such as mastering various reading skills? If not, does the technology deliver results that are superior to corresponding alternatives for a comparable investment? For example, if a district chose to invest in staff development aimed at improving teachers' reading instruction, would students in those classrooms make smaller or larger gains than those in classrooms where an ILS system was installed? Does the district introduce such programs as pilots, allowing for comparisons and reviews of costs and benefits? Is the data from such studies made available to the board as part of the district decision-making process?

12. IS THE DISTRICT EVALUATING WHAT IS HAPPENING?

excellent (5)   good (4)   fair (3)   weak (2)   poor (1)

Related Questions: What kinds of data are gathered to assess the impact of various technologies? Is the data gathered in an objective fashion, following accepted principles for experimental design to avoid bias? Does the evaluation design take into account issues such as the "Hawthorne effect" and the differential impact of volunteers as implementers of pilot programs? Is data used formatively, as a guide to future decisions and program modifications?

13. IS THE TECHNOLOGY EFFICIENT, FLEXIBLE, ADAPTABLE, AND CURRENT?

excellent (5)   good (4)   fair (3)   weak (2)   poor (1)

Related Questions: Are issues such as processing speed, expandability and connectivity addressed in district planning and purchasing? If students will be using the technology to do graphics or CAD, for example, do cost considerations result in the purchase of low-speed technology that will require students to sit and stare at the screen for minutes at a time, wasting many hours over the course of a year? Do similar considerations result in the purchase of black-and-white monitors, which limit the ability of students to work in 3-D or work with multiple variables in graphing and statistics programs? When videodisc players, CD-ROM players, computers, video cameras, etc., are purchased, are choices made with a 3- to 5-year perspective? Are models with maximal expandability and adaptability selected to protect against premature obsolescence? Is obsolescent existing technology maintained far past program usefulness because it has not stopped working? What planning procedures are in place to provide for timely updating of technologies and the transfer of obsolescent equipment to programs where the shortcomings are irrelevant?

TOTAL SCORE_____

55-65 = outstanding

45-55 = strong

45 or less indicates a need for improvement

CHAPTER SEVENTEEN

OPEN-MINDED SCHOOL DECISION-MAKING

INTRODUCTION: AN OPEN MIND DEFINED

A mind that welcomes new ideas.

A mind that invites new ideas for a visit.

A mind that introduces new ideas to the company that already has arrived.

A mind that is most comfortable in mixed company.

A mind that prizes silence and reflection.

A mind that recognizes that later is often better than sooner.

A major premise of collaborative problem-solving is that the combined thinking of several minds is likely to produce richer, better, and wiser solutions than does solitary thinking. For this premise to prove true, the participants must be open-minded. They must believe that they have much to learn from each other.

- *An open mind is somewhat like silly putty.* Do you remember that wonderful ball of soft substance that you could bounce, roll, and apply to comics as a child?

- *An open mind is playful and willing to be silly* because the best ideas often hide deep within our minds, away from our watchful, judgmental selves. Although our

141

personalities contain the conflicting voices of both a clown and a critic, the critic usually prevails in our culture, especially when we attend meetings. The critic's voice keeps warning us not to appear foolish in front of our peers, not to offer up any outrageous ideas; yet, that is precisely how we get with the most inventive and imaginative solutions to problems. We need to learn how to lock up the critic at times so the clown can play without restraint. We must prevent our internal critic from blocking our own thinking or attacking the ideas of others. We must join in creating a meeting climate that supports wild and wonderful thinking, free of risk. Once we have generated a rich menu of options, then we can release the critic to help us with the planning and implementation phases. Roger von Oech's two books, *A Whack on the Side of the Head* (1990) and *A Kick in the Seat of the Pants* (1986), are excellent sources of exercises to loosen up one's innovative powers and release the mental locks.

- *An open mind can bounce around* in what often might seem like a haphazard fashion. When building something new, we must be willing to entertain unusual combinations and connections. The human mind, at its best, is especially powerful in jumping intuitively to discover unusual relationships and possibilities. Trainers in group process often use forced metaphors to provoke unusual thinking, for example, asking a group to consider how a principal in the Information Age might be like a dancer. Synthesis requires fanciful recombination of elements over and over until at least one combination unlocks the puzzle and gives the group what is most needed. Because *brainstorming* (idea generation) often is constrained in our culture by the overly healthy critics sitting inside each participant, it takes a good bit of work to warm up the group and provoke ideas that are truly novel and "outside the box."

- *An open mind quickly picks up the good ideas of other people,* much like silly putty copying the image from a page of colored comics. The open mind is always hungry, looking for some new thoughts to add to its collection. The open mind knows that its own thinking is almost always incomplete. An open mind takes pride in learning from others. It would rather listen than speak. It loves to ask questions like, "How did you come up with that idea? Can you tell me more about your thinking? How did you know that? What are your premises? What evidence did you find?"

- *The open mind has "in-sight,"* evaluating the quality of its own thinking to see gaps which might be filled. The open mind trains the clown and the critic to cooperate, so that judgment and critique alternate with playful idea generation. Ideas have at least three major aspects that can be modified and improved:

    1. *Ideas are based on premises* of one kind or another. Many people come to their ideas (judgments or conclusions) without ever explicitly examining the premises that lie underneath those conclusions. Premises are basic beliefs. In planning schools of the future, for example, members of a team might hold as a premise that students learn best when they have as much formal direct instructional time in classrooms as possible. If that premise controls much of their thinking about the future, huge menus of exciting possibilities are immediately excluded from thinking. Collections of premises often are called assumptions or mind-sets (Drucker, 1992) or paradigms (Barker, 1992) or mental models (Senge, 1991). Sometimes our thinking comes to

us already packaged, without our even knowing which premises and assumptions lie below the surface. But an open mind knows that all such premises must be re-examined with some frequency to see if they are serving us well and truly match our basic belief systems.

2. *Ideas are based on evidence.* Many of our ideas emerge from experience. We collect data, look for patterns, and seek laws to help us predict the future. For example, if we believe that tracking is not the best way to organize a school, we probably have been collecting examples of ways that students have suffered from such a system. We probably have been doing some professional reading to provide additional evidence from research to support our idea. We also have been speaking with colleagues who are similarly inclined.

Unfortunately, all too often we collect evidence selectively. Research has shown that once people begin to hold an idea, they begin to screen out data that might create dissonance, evidence that might "call into question" the value of the idea. Knowing that a particular faction of the faculty loves tracking, for example, opponents of tracking are not likely to sit around and hold thoughtful, considerate discussions to understand how these others came to their own conclusions (unless, of course, they have open minds). Scanning the shelves of a bookstore, the opponents of tracking are likely to pick out the title supporting their view. A book supporting tracking goes unnoticed (unless, of course, they have open minds and know that their own thinking will be strengthened by reviewing *all* of the evidence).

An open mind looks at the quality of its evidence with the same dispassionate attitude it applies to its premises and assumptions. The open mind asks, "What evidence do I need to gather? Do I know enough? Has anything changed since I last gathered evidence? Is there new data? Is my data complete?"

3. *Ideas are based on logic.* Our conclusions and ideas should flow from logical connections between our premises and our evidence. For example, when considering the choice of a teaching strategy such as *cooperative learning* for a particular new program, we should have employed the skills that Bloom (1954) labeled "evaluation." The logic of this process requires that we compare and contrast the features of several different teaching strategies, collecting data to assess the relative worth of each, as judged in terms of explicitly stated criteria. Having applied this kind of reasoning and logic to the task, we seek to predict what student outcomes will best be served by implementing cooperative learning. All too often, groups and individuals jump to solutions without identifying the real problem or fully considering all of the available options; but an open-minded group takes the time to employ a careful decision-making model, which will require full, logical analysis. The open mind keeps asking of its ideas, "Is this logical? Does this make sense? Does this follow from the evidence I gathered? Have I identified all the key factors?"

WHAT IS A CLOSED MIND?

A mind that is "made up."

Closed-minded people come to meetings to fight for their position and their ideas. They see meetings as contests and struggles. If a faculty is divided into factions of closed-minded people, meetings are spent attacking and undermining the ideas of others in order to win support (and votes) for one's own idea. The critics are set free with well-sharpened blades.

In *The Fifth Discipline,* Senge (1990) argues that most organizations suffer from adversarial exchanges and closed-mindedness at meetings. A typical meeting runs for hours without anybody bothering to ask a question to increase under-standing of other people's thinking. Senge labels such exchanges as *discussion,* which is basically argumentative. He stresses the importance of teaching groups to engage in far more *dialogue* to balance the discussion. *Dialogue* is the team exploration of ideas in an open-minded fashion, with all assumptions suspended. Groups should be good at both kinds of exchanges, knowing when each is appropriate. *Dialogue* (basically divergent) is especially good for generating possibili-ties and enhancing understanding. *Discussion* (basically con-vergent) works best when it is time to select from the menu and begin to plan action.

> *In dialogue, individuals gain insights that simply could not be achieved individually. A new kind of mind comes into being which is based on the development of a common meaning . . . People are no longer primarily in opposition, nor can they be said to be interacting, rather they are participating in this pool of common meaning, which is capable of constant development and change.*
>
> *In dialogue, a group explores complex issues from many points of view. Individuals suspend their assumptions but they communicate their assumptions freely (p. 240).*

Closed minds are fond of auto-pilot and tradition. They love to look back at old track records, confident that what worked yesterday will endure tomorrow. They have ceased learning. They try to ignore what has happened to the American steel industry and automobile industry. They see no lessons to be learned from IBM and Sears. "This could never happen to us," they whisper.

Closed-mindedness is extremely dangerous in times of rapid change and turbulence. Trailing-edge practice soon becomes failing-edge practice, as outmoded thinking translates into poor performance and obsolescence. Skeptics were quick to warn Columbus that he would fall off the edge of the earth if he followed his pioneering instincts, but he could have warned them that they might fall off an edge themselves if the world kept turning and they failed to move with the times. They were warning him about the leading (or bleeding) edge. He might warn them of the trailing edge.

> We trap ourselves, say Argyris and his colleagues, in "defensive routines" that insulate our mental models from examination, and we consequently develop "skilled incompetence," a marvelous oxymoron that Argyris uses to describe most adult learners, who are highly skillful at protecting themselves from pain and threat posed by learning situations, but consequently fail to learn how to produce the results they really want. (Senge, p. 182)

Open-Mindedness and School Restructuring

Some proponents of site-based decision-making and restructuring—especially legislators who have passed mandates with inadequate funding for staff development—have a naive conception of how little a lifetime spent in schools prepares one for successful group problem-solving. While the premises of site-based decision-making seem to make a good deal of sense, these legislators have assumed too much about the readiness of the participants to assume the new responsibilities imposed on them. It may be that the richness of ideas applied to school planning can be improved by involving a broader group. It may be that the appropriateness of the ideas can be improved by involving those closest to the children (clients). It may be that staff ownership of initiatives can be enhanced if they are given a greater voice in the making of decisions. But all of those premises depend on the ability of the groups to function in an open-minded, productive fashion and avoid two especially big temptations.

TEMPTATION #1—PLAYING IT SAFE

Chapter 15 explored how change often is slowed by the wish of individuals and groups to remain within the *comfort zone*. Harmony may be held in greater esteem than innovation. Risk and adventure may be seen as threatening. Security and stability may be the priority. Paradigm paralysis may rule the day. It is sad that Sears closed more than a hundred stores because it could not see the writing on the wall and learn to invent a new kind of successful store. Its decades of success contributed to its demise. The formulas that served so well for so long became dogma. For the same reasons, school planning groups may opt for "first-order change" (tinkering with minor adjustments) rather than second-order change (major shifts in the mission and delivery systems).

TEMPTATION #2—LOCKING THE GRID

Much of our culture leads toward conflict, positions, and adversarial exchanges. If we are not taught conflict resolution and the kinds of team learning strategies advocated by Senge (1990) and others, we all too often find ourselves locked in place, fighting over several different plans. Meetings become divisive, exhausting, and destructive. Morale plummets. Many participants begin to request a return to hierarchical, autocratic leadership, giving up in disgust on a group process that leads nowhere.

The best way to avoid the problems listed above is to invest in training to shift the culture of schools from isolation to collaboration. Joyce and Showers' (1983, 1988, 1990) work on staff development outlines in some detail how to lead a school or district through such a cultural transformation.

The "guide on the side" rather than the "sage on the stage." Some of the same practices that support open-minded group discussion also support inquiry teaching, since a class becomes a group or cluster of groups all exploring essential questions. The sage hands over expertise, ideas that are cultural artifacts. The guide hands over tools and shows students how to wield them in powerful ways.

In some organizations, employees are expected to embrace change. Adaptability becomes part of the performance evaluation. In such organizations, no one is allowed to fold their arms and exercise veto power over change initiatives. No one is allowed to "bail out." If they truly want "out," they must find a new job. No dragging of heels or sabotage is tolerated. No patient waiting for retirement.

I went into a Sears to buy an electric blanket a few months back. It was a good sale and a good price. As I lined up at the register to pay, I took out my wallet and handed the clerk a charge card.

"Oh," she said, "we only accept a Sears charge card."

Short on cash, I put my wallet away.

"We would be glad to open a charge account for you tonight and let you buy the blanket with your new card," she urged.

"No thanks," I replied, heading for the door. On the way out, I wondered who was the mental giant who came up with that policy. How many other customers had they lost in the same way? What would it take to get them to change course, to challenge their mental models?

Open-Mindedness and Technology Planning

Great technology planning requires a truly open mind, willing to entertain fundamental shifts in the ways, times, and places that learning takes place. To tap the fullest potential of new technologies, planning groups must set aside schooling as it has been and consider very different scenarios. Unfortunately, this kind of thinking may prove threatening to sages and those unwilling to adapt. These members of a planning group may argue for a strategic approach, building incrementally on the schooling practices already in place. Keeping their noses to the ground, they build technological systems that are archaic before they are installed. For these groups, decisions about technology concern only hardware and software. Pedagogy and andragogy go unexamined.

What about Apple's *Newton,* for example? How many district technology planning committees have asked how to tap its potential? All too often, we plan for how to use only the hardware that is on the market when the plan is being written.

Borrowing from the work of Davis (1987) and Schwartz (1991), I suggest a technology planning model that includes scenario building and open-mindedness.

Imagine a group of teachers developing and then sharing their own "future perfect" scenarios in an open-minded fashion. A good scenario, according to Schwartz, helps us to think about what might otherwise be considered unthinkable. It helps us to leap beyond our standard ways of thinking and entertain far more futures.

Conclusion: Final Ironies

Even though we are in a learning profession, for too long schools have been structured in ways that isolate teachers from one another, enforce hierarchical controls, and engender closed-mindedness. Now we suddenly are thrust into the TQM and site-based decision-making models as the latest in a long string of fads to pass through our business (often from the outside) with little consideration of the educational context and its readiness for such models. Few resources exist in most school districts to build the organizational culture and skills that would support the kind of team decision-making and adult learning envisioned by Senge; thus these fads are likely to have as much impact as did the dozen reform initiatives that preceded them. Schools must invest heavily in human resource development and new communication structures if change in practice and group decision-making are to flourish.

CHAPTER EIGHTEEN

THE FINE ART OF PARADIGM BUSTING AND FLEXADIGM BREEDING

INTRODUCTION

Routine is the enemy of invention. Like deer who will follow the same path to a watering hole even after construction begins on an Interstate and even after the semi-trailers begin roaring down the highway, we often allow our habits to govern behaviors long after those patterns have proven ineffective, wrong-minded, or dangerous.

The routines, patterns, and scripts we follow derive from mind-sets and belief systems that are deeply embedded, often submerged below consciousness. These deeply held values and attitudes dictate our actions, even though they may conflict with the professed or public belief system. That is the case for organizations, as well as individuals, as in the case of schools that claim to encourage each student to reach his or her fullest potential but actually devote great energy to sorting, sifting, and tracking students by race or socioeconomic status.

Successful adaptation to a turbulent, changing world requires the open exploration and re-examination of these mind-sets so that they will cease to command actions unconsciously, automatically, and inappropriately. The healthy organization is wary of mind-sets, because they are too much like concrete; they do not bend well.

We must develop skill at *Paradigm busting*—the process of re-examining old mind-sets and operating systems to determine whether they should still serve as governing principles. *Paradigm busting* is actually an early stage of *flexadigm breeding*. We must open up the way individual and collective minds think about the way business is conducted, children are educated, and futures are created. Once the collective mind is open, fresh thinking becomes natural. We develop an organizational culture that encourages new growth.

Schools: A Lack of Innovation Infrastructure

Schools possess little innovation infrastructure. If one were to design an organization ill-disposed to change, one might employ the following recipe:

- Isolate all of the employees from each other so that there is virtually no opportunity for planning, discussion, or group problem-solving.

- Isolate the employees from the outside world and insulate them from new developments, trends, and opportunities.

- Load the employees with tasks that consume most of their waking hours and make reflection an impossible dream.

- Stress the importance of routines, policies, and manuals.

- Impose significant penalties for taking risks. Reward compliance.

- Treat as heretics those employees who question authority and routines.

- Provide no resources for learning, research, and organizational development.

154

Just as communication and transportation systems serve as critically important infrastructure for the economy and society at large, healthy organizations require major investments in structures and systems that encourage innovative thinking and inventive adaptation to changing conditions.

In preparing students for the next century, school districts might consider how to establish the kind of organizational culture that engenders open-mindedness and imaginative thinking, replacing the recipe listed above with the following precepts:

- Build 10 hours or more into each work week during which teachers and other staff members can meet with each other or work with each other on planning, discussion, and group problem-solving. Provide significant summer time (2 or more weeks) for staff development, curriculum development, and school restructuring activities.

- Establish idea conduits, linking staff with the most promising ideas and most important trends emerging from the outside world. Provide every staff member with access to print and electronic journals, bulletin boards, and conferencing of various kinds. Connect with the global electronic highway so that the world's information resources are a mouse-click away.

- Re-examine duties assigned to staff and reduce tedious, repetitious, non-professional tasks, such as paperwork and baby-sitting, in favor of invention, planning, communication, and collaboration. Build reflection into the work day.

- Stress the importance of adaptation, imagination, responsiveness, and innovation within the parameters of the district mission statement.

- Reward reasonable risk-taking and growth. Provide support and protection to the risk-takers. Clarify expectations for those who refuse to grow or change.

- Treat employees who question authority and routines—responsibly—as heroes and pioneers. Reward paradigm busting and flexadigm breeding.

- Provide generous resources for learning, research, and organizational development.

This list will seem like pie-in-the-sky to most school people. The vision represents such a fundamental shift in the nature of the organization that it is hard to believe in its plausibility. However, colleges and universities routinely provide faculty with many of the resources listed above, freeing teachers from custodial chores and distilling formal instruction into brief episodes.

The biggest barriers to the kind of organization envisioned above are K-12 paradigms about time, learning, and the purpose of schooling. For example:

OLD PARADIGM—PURPOSE OF SCHOOLING

While the public or professed purpose of schools is the development of competent young citizens and workers, a long-standing, unspoken purpose is custodial care. Especially as social trends require most parents to work outside the home, the school is seen as a major provider of daycare.

Why is this a barrier to change? Those who try to provide staff development by sending students home early will face stiff parental and community opposition. Any redesign of schooling that sends children back into the community ahead of schedule will draw fire. If anything, most of the current pressure is to provide longer school days and years, with the ultimate (undesirable) model being a boarding school for elementary students.

The challenge facing schools today is to find ways of providing custodial care while releasing the professional staff from obligations to provide such service. It is far too costly to assign highly trained teachers to such chores. It makes better sense to bring in paraprofessionals for such duties.

OLD PARADIGM—LEARNING

One paradigm blocking much restructuring is the belief that student learning is best promoted by increasing the number of hours of formal contact between teachers and students in classrooms. When we watch what happens during many of those hours, it is clear that many of the activities are custodial in nature, requiring little real professionalism. The solution is "instructional compacting," a strategy that places students in formal, large-group contact with teachers for fewer hours each week in order to deliver carefully distilled lessons in a highly efficient manner. Students would spend the rest of the school time working on research, projects, and assignments that can be handled with considerable independence under the watchful and supportive eyes of paraprofessionals teamed with specialists.

Talk of differentiated staffing raises the specter of staff reductions. With considerable justification, teachers fear that fewer class hours will mean fewer teacher jobs, since there is little reason to expect that financially hard-pressed communities will entertain the belief that student learning will increase if teachers have more time to think, plan, learn, and collaborate. Yet, because this topic has long been taboo, schools can do little to break the organizational gridlock posed by inadequate professional time for growth.

With the advent of new technologies, there will be vastly improved opportunities for students to work individually and in groups without constant teacher supervision. We must seize the opportunity to free teachers to serve an increasingly tutorial and inventive role. We also must let go of time-honored staffing patterns, which begin to resemble the feather-bedding that undermined the competitiveness of the railroad industry. Master teachers should be required for intensely interactive exchanges with challenging instructional demands, not assigned to monitor study halls or seat work.

SCHOOLS AS LEARNING ORGANIZATIONS

Because paradigm shifters—the ones who first challenge the old paradigm's usefulness—are often viewed as renegades or heretics by the organization, it pays to institutionalize the paradigm busting process, so that the responsibility is shared by the entire group. Shared decision-making and system-wide paradigm busting is the "path of least resistance." When only isolated individuals criticize, express doubt, and judge the old ways and old mind-sets negatively, they are likely to set in motion defensive routines and mechanisms that will inhibit learning. The energy of the organization goes into protecting the *status quo*. It is more productive to enlist all members of the group in the learning process.

Peter Senge's *The Fifth Discipline: The Art and Practice of the Learning Organization* (1990) provides an excellent description of four core disciplines necessary for an organization's commitment to a systems perspective:

1. ***Personal Mastery***—Senge argues that resistance to change usually results from individual discomfort with what he calls "creative tension," which "often leads to feelings or emotions associated with anxiety, such as sadness, discouragement, hopelessness, or worry" (p. 151). The health of the organization ultimately depends on the strengthening of individual capacities to endure such tension.

2. ***Mental Mastery***—This discipline involves group members in surfacing the mental models (mind-sets or paradigms) that dictate much of the organizational behavior,

so they can be re-examined and adapted. Participants become model-builders, shaping the operating systems of the organization to fit the demands of a changing world. If all members of the group are engaged in the search for useful models, outmoded models are likely to drop away.

3. *Shared Vision*—Senge emphasizes the value of a vision constructed from the individual visions of group members, rather than handed down from the top of a hierarchy. He describes the difference between commitment and enrollment, where participants invest their selves in the journey, and compliance, where people may go along with reluctance and dragging feet.

4. *Team Learning*—Senge stresses the importance of teaching groups to work open-mindedly together, exploring ideas and possibilities as well as arguing about them. He differentiates between *discussion,* which is generally adversarial, and *dialogue,* which is collaborative. Discussion predominates in most groups, with people taking positions, defending those positions, and attacking the positions of other factions. Dialogue is rare and counter-cultural. Open-minded exploration involves a "suspension of assumptions," while members of the group help each other extend their thinking and their insight. People come to meetings knowing they will leave better informed than they were when they arrived.

The first step in paradigm busting, then, is the creation of a learning culture, one in which questioning how we go about educating children becomes routine. Asking how we might improve quality becomes a daily challenge.

ISSUES OF SCALE, CHOICE, AND HETEROGENEITY

Because it is questionable whether groups can achieve passionate visions when hundreds of staff members must participate in the dialogue, districts may have to assign far more decision-making responsibility to small groups, as is being tried in the Philadelphia system with charter "schools within schools"—200 to 400 students with 10 to 12 teachers operating semi-autonomously. This promising initiative, sponsored by the Pew Charitable Trust, places the responsibility for invention where it belongs, with the classroom teacher; but it does so with groups that can form a consensus around key values and can develop a program with strong appeal and identity, one which is not a mish-mash or disappointing amalgam of conflicting perspectives.

With the arrival of the Clinton Administration, public school choice is likely to replace voucher systems as the hot reform topic. Instead of planning school programs so as to accommodate or appease all the various factions that might make up a typical faculty, public school choice allows each faction to build programs around passionately held belief systems and then identify students and families who find the resulting offerings attractive, appealing, and convincing.

REACHING THE BREAKING POINT

In *Breakpoint and Beyond: Mastering the Future—Today,* Land and Jarman (1992) warn that organizations are facing a different kind of change, which may not allow for smooth transitions and evolutionary adjustments:

> *The entire notion of change turns out to be amazingly different from what we have long thought it to be. Change actually follows a pattern that results in momentous and seemingly unpredictable shifts. Long periods of great disorder can shift abruptly to regularity, stability, and predictability. Equally long periods of incremental, continuous, and logical advancement shift to an entirely different kind of change—one in which unrelated things combine in creative ways that produce unexpected and powerful results.*

160

> *At breakpoint, the rule change is so sharp that continuing to use the old rules not only doesn't work, [but] it erects great, sometimes insurmountable barriers to success.* (Quoted in *Training & Development*, November, 1992, p. 79)

Examples of breakpoints for the educational world may be the sudden reduction of school funding in states like California, the sudden redesign of school finance in New Jersey, the arrival of a private educational corporation to run schools in Baltimore, waves of Third World students in a particular state or region, or the introduction of new technologies that replace brick schools with electronic, home schooling.

School districts that invest in organizational development to create learning organizations will suffer the fewest dislocations and traumas when breaking points arrive, because they will have the ability to adjust and adapt while rule-oriented, hierarchical structures provide too little flexibility. Instead of bending when the heavy winds strike, old structures are likely to break.

NEW BEGINNINGS

John Rollwagen (1992), CEO for Cray Research, manufacturer of the world's most powerful supercomputers, stresses the importance of everybody being a "constant beginner." He tells the story of how company founder, Seymour Cray, used to build wonderful wooden boats each year, sail them for a summer, and then hold a party to burn each boat so that a new one could be built that winter. Each boat was followed by a better one. "He was a constant, constant beginner" (p. 32).

He quotes from Rilke:

> *If the angel deigns to come, it will be*
> *because you have convinced her not by your tears*
> *but by your humble resolve to be always beginning,*
> *to be a beginner.*

We often are reluctant to start schools from scratch, burning our boats behind us; and yet many of the most exciting and innovative programs in the United States engage teachers in exactly such new beginnings. Adjusting existing schools is very different than creating new ones with groups of teachers unified by a common vision. Incremental adjustments all too often are hampered by paradigms that have ceased to serve the best interests of either teachers or students.

FUTURE SCENARIOS

Those who would test the potential of new technologies to elevate the reasoning powers of all students and create student-centered learning will find countless obstacles placed in their path by those who would just as soon proceed with business as usual. As Cuban (1992) notes, the "technophile's dream: electronic schools of the future now," is the least likely scenario for this decade. He identifies existing mind-sets and paradigms as the main reason for a much slower acceptance of new technologies:

> *The sparing classroom use of computers is due less to inadequate funds, unprepared teachers, and indifferent administrators and more to dominant cultural beliefs about what teaching, learning and proper knowledge are and to the age-graded school with its self-contained classrooms, time schedules, and fragmented curriculum.* (p. 27)

While Cuban predicts slow acceptance of new technologies and "the spread of hybrids of teacher-centered and student-centered instruction," he acknowledges such wild cards as the movement for national standards and the growing privatization of public schools as forces that could upset his predictions (p. 27).

Cuban's article documents the lamentable co-opting of new technologies by old educational mind-sets. Despite hundreds of

162

millions of dollars invested in hardware, the regular classroom has changed little in most places. We have our hybrids and our hothouses, but the potential of all this equipment to transform schooling and learning has been blunted by the momentum of old paradigms. Transformation and restructuring require the development of new structures in schools that empower teachers to explore, invent, and challenge.

It is time for schools to be the way they are meant to be.

REFERENCES

American Association for the Advancement of Science. (1989). *Science for all Americans: summary, Project 2061.* Washington, D.C.

Apple Computer, (1990). *Macintosh writing resource guide.* Cupertino, CA.

Applebee, A. *et. al.* (1986). The writing report card: writing achievement in American schools. Princeton, NJ: Educational Testing Service.

Argyris, C. (1990). *Overcoming Organizational Defenses.* New York: Prentice-Hall.

Barker, J. (1992). *Future edge: discovering the new paradigms of success.* New York: William Morrow and Company, Inc.

Becker, H. (1987). The impact of computer use on children's learning: what research has shown and what it has not. Paper presented at the Annual Meeting of the American Educational Research Association, Washington, DC, April 20-24.

Becker, H. (1988, November). The impact of computer use on children's learning. *Principal.*

Becker, H. (1991). How computers are used in United States schools: basic data from the 1989 I.E.A. computers in education survey. *Journal of Educational Computing Research,* 4, pp. 385-406.

Becker, H. (1991). Mathematics and science uses of computers in American schools, 1989. *Journal of Computers in Mathematics and Science Teaching*; 4, pp.19-25.

Becker, H. (1991). When powerful tools meet conventional beliefs and institutional restraints. *Computing Teacher*; 8, pp. 6-9.

Becker, H. (1991). Encyclopedias on CD-ROM: two orders of magnitude more than any other educational software has ever delivered before. *Educational Technology*; 2, pp.7-20.

Bents, R. and Howey, K. (1981). Staff development— change in the individual. In Staff development—organization development. Edited by B. Day. Alexandria, VA: ASCD.

Beyer, Francine S. (1992, March). *Impact of computers on middle-level student writing skills.* Paper presented at AERA, April 20-24. Philadelphia, PA: Research for Better Schools.

Bloom, B. (1954). *Taxonomy of educational objectives. Handbook I: cognitive domain.* New York: Longmans, Green & Co.

Bradley, A. (1992, November 18) Reforming Philadelphia's high schools from within. *Education Week*, pp. 1, 17-19.

Campbell, J. with Moyers, W. (1988). *The Power of Myth.* New York: Doubleday.

Campbell, D. and Stanley, J. (1963). Experimental and quasi-experimental designs for research. Chicago: Rand McNally.

Catford, L. and Ray, M. (1991). *The path of the everyday hero.* Los Angeles: Jeremy P. Tarcher, Inc.

Comer, J. (1992). Organize Schools around Child Development. *Social Policy*; 3, pp. 28-30.

Cuban, L. (1992, November 11). Computers meet classroom; classroom wins. *Education Week*, pp. 36, 27.

Davidow, W. and Uttal, B. (1989). New York: Harper Perennial.

Davis, S. (1987). *Future perfect.* Reading, MA: Addison-Wesley Publishing Company, Inc.

Davis, S. and Davidson, W. (1991). *2020 vision: transforming your business today to succeed in tomorrow's economy.* New York: Simon & Schuster.

Drucker, P. (1985). *Innovation and entrepreneurship: practices and principles.* New York: Harper and Row.

Drucker, P. (1992). *Managing for the future.* New York: Truman Talley Books.

Eisner, E. (1991). What Really Counts in Schools. *Educational Leadership*; 5, pp. 10-11,14-17.

Frye, S. (1989, May). The NCTM standards—challenges for all classrooms. *Arithmetic Teacher*, 9, pp. 4-7.

Fullan, M. (1991). *The new meaning of educational change.* New York: Teachers College Press.

Garson, B. (1988). *The electronic sweatshop.* New York: Penguin.

Goldberg, M. (1984, January) An update on the National Writing Project. *Phi Delta Kappan*; 5, pp. 356-57.

Goodlad, J. (1984). *A place called school.* Hightstown, NJ: McGraw-Hill.

Hunt, D. (1971). *Matching models in education.* Toronto: Ontario Institute for Studies in Education.

Hyman, R. (1980). Fielding Student Questions. *Theory into Practice*; 1, pp. 38-44.

Jones, L., et. al. (1992). The 1990 science report card. NAEP's assessment of fourth, eighth, and twelfth graders. Princeton, NJ: Educational Testing Service.

Joyce, B. and Showers, B. (1983). *Power in staff development through research in training.* Alexandria, VA: ASCD.

Joyce, Bruce R. (1988) *Student achievement through staff development.* White Plains, NY: Longman.

Joyce, B. (Ed). (1990). *Changing school culture through staff development*. Alexandria, VA: ASCD.

Kanter, R. (1983). *The change masters*. New York: Simon and Schuster.

Kulik, J. and Kulik, C. (1989, Spring). Effectiveness of computer-based instruction. *School Library Media Quarterly*.

Kulik, J. and Kulik, C. (1991). Effectiveness of computer-based instruction: an updated analysis. *Computers in Human Behavior*, 7, p. 91.

Land, G. and Jarman, B. (1992). *Breakpoint and beyond: mastering the future—today*. New York: HarperBusiness.

Mandinach, E. (1992). The impact of technological innovation on teaching and learning activities. Paper presented at AERA annual meeting.

McKenzie, J. (1991). *Site-based decision-making: a practical guide for practitioners*. Flemington, NJ: Correct Change Press.

Melville, H. (1942). *Moby Dick*. Syracuse, NY: L. W. Singer Co.

Michalko, M. (1991). *Thinkertoys*. Berkeley: Ten Speed Press.

Mojkowski, Charles, and Bamberger, R. (1991, March). Developing leaders for restructuring schools. A Report of the National LEADership Network Study Group on Restructuring Schools. Office of Educational Research and Improvement (ED), Washington, DC. Programs for the Improvement of Practice. Report No.: PIP-91-824.

Morton, M. (ed.) (1991). *The Corporation of the 1990s*. New York: Oxford University Press.

NAEP (National Assessment of Educational Progress)

New York City Public Schools. (1990, April). Evaluation of the Writing to Read Program. Brooklyn, NY: Office of Research, Evaluation, and Assessment.

Olson, L. (1992, October 7). New approaches blurring the line between public and private schools. *Education Week*: 5, pp. 1, 18-21.

Owston, R. (1990). On and off computer writing of eighth grade students experienced in word processing. Technical report 90-1. York University, North York (Ontario). Centre for the Study of Computers in Education. May. ERIC abstract ED319053.

Peters, T. (1987). *Thriving on chaos*. New York: Alfred A. Knopf.

Popcorn, F. (1991). *The popcorn report*. New York: Doubleday.

Polya, G. (1963). Studies in mathematics, Volume XI: mathematical methods in science. Stanford Univ., Calif. School Mathematics Study Group.

Postman, N. (1992). *Technopoly*. New York: Alfred A. Knopf.

Reich, R. (1991). *The work of nations: preparing ourselves for 21st century capitalism*. New York: Alfred A. Knopf.

Renzulli, J. et. al. (1983). Curriculum compacting: an essential strategy for working with gifted students. *Gifted Education International*; 2 pp. 97-102.

Rollwagen, J. (1992, November). *Training and Development*, pp. 30-38.

Schwartz, P. (1991). *The art of the long view*. New York: Doubleday-Currency.

Sculley, J. with Byrne, J. (1987). *Odyssey*. New York: Harper & Row.

Senge, P. (1990). *The fifth discipline: the art and practice of the learning organization*. New York: Doubleday/Currency.

Simon, P. (1991). Kodachrome™. From Paul Simon's concert in the park. BMI.

Sizer, T. (1984). *Horace's compromise*. Boston: Houghton Mifflin Company.

Sizer, T. (1992). *Horace's school*. Boston: Houghton Mifflin Company.

Sprinthall, N. and Sprinthall, L. (1980). Adult development and leadership training for mainstream education. In *Concepts to guide the training of teachers of teachers*. Edited by D. Corrigan and K. Howey. Reston, Virginia: Council for Exceptional Children .

Toffler, A. (1990). *Power Shift*. New York: Bantam Books.

Tucker, R. (1991). *Managing the future: 10 driving forces of change for the 90s*. New York: G.P. Putnam's Sons.

Vaill, P. (1989). *Managing as a performing art: new ideas for a world of chaotic change*. San Francisco: Jossey-Bass, Inc. Publishers.

von Oech, R. (1990). *A whack on the side of the head*. New York: Warner Books.

von Oech, R. (1986). *A kick in the seat of the pants*. New York: Harper & Row.

White, M. (1984). The electronic learning revolution: questions we should be asking. *Prospects: Quarterly Review of Education*, 1, 23-33.

Wilson, K. (1992). Two multimedia design research projects: Palenque and The Museum Visitor's Project. Technical Report No. 23. Center for Technology in Education, New York, NY.

Zuboff, S. (1988). *In the age of the smart machine*. New York: Basic Books.

DID YOU KNOW THAT WE OFFER PROFESSIONAL DEVELOPMENT WORKSHOPS?

The National Educational Service has a strong commitment to enhancing the lives of youth by producing top-quality, timely materials for the professionals who work with them. Our resource materials include books, videos, and professional development workshops in the following areas:

Discipline with Dignity

Reclaiming Youth at Risk

Cooperative Learning

Thinking Across the Curriculum

Cooperative Management

Parental Involvement

Our current mission focuses on celebrating diversity in the classroom and managing change in education.

DO YOU HAVE AN IDEA TO SHARE?

We are always looking for high-quality manuscripts that are designed for educators and others who work with youth. We welcome project proposals from dynamic writers and speakers who are interested in spreading the word about new, innovative, or especially effective approaches to timely issues in education. Our publications are research-based, yet written in an accessible style, and generally emphasize practical applications.

For more information about our other products and services, or to receive detailed submission guidelines, please contact:

Nancy Shin, Director of Publications
National Educational Service
1610 West Third Street
P.O. Box 8
Bloomington, IN 47402
1-800-733-6786
1-812-336-7700

NEED MORE COPIES?

Need more copies of this book? Want your own copy? If so, you can order additional copies of *Administrators At Risk: Tools and Technologies for Securing Your Future* by using this form or by calling us at (800) 733-6786 (US only) or (812) 336-7700. Or you can order by FAX at (812) 336-7790.

We guarantee complete satisfaction with all of our materials. If you are not completely satisfied with any NES publication, you may return it to us within 30 days for a full refund.

	Quantity	Total Price
Administrators At Risk: Tools and Technologies for Securing Your Future ($19.95 each)	_____	_____
Shipping: Add $2.00 per copy (There is no shipping charge when you *include* payment with your order.)		_____
Indiana residents add 5% sales tax		_____
TOTAL		_____

❏ Check enclosed with order   ❏ Money Order
❏ Please bill me (P.O. #_____)
❏ VISA or MasterCard
Account No._____ Exp. Date _____
Cardholder _____
Ship to:
Name_____ Title _____
Organization_____
Address _____
City_____ State_____ ZIP_____
Phone_____ FAX _____

MAIL TO:
National Educational Service
1610 West Third Street
P.O. Box 8
Bloomington, IN 47402

WHAT ARE THE EXPERTS SAYING ABOUT *ADMINISTRATORS AT RISK: TOOLS AND TECHNOLOGIES FOR SECURING YOUR FUTURE?*

*"**McKenzie has laid out a blueprint** for operating a twenty-first century school....Any educator who wants to do a good job, or simply survive into the next decade, should read, study, and implement the concepts in this book."*

— from the foreword by Michael F. Sullivan
Executive Director
Association for Instructional Technology

*"Provocative...fast-paced...**very current and relevant**."*

— Donna Rhodes
Executive Director
National Foundation for the
Improvement of Education

*"Provides **innovative ideas** about strategies for enhancing the richness of a learning community for students and faculty."*

— Cory Walden
Academic Coordinator
Upward Bound Program
University of Maryland

*"A **must read** for anyone struggling with the role of technology in schools."*

— Richard DuFour
Superintendent
Lincolnshire, IL

*"Has taken many ideas from different educational circles and put them into a **workable, practical application**."*

— Peter Domenici
Principal
Wilmington, OH

ISBN 1-879639-27-0